MW00574436

Setting Boundaries®
with Your Adult Children
Companion Study Guide

❧

SANITY Support Group
Workbook & Leader Guide

Allison **Bottke**

Fort Worth, Texas

Setting Boundaries® with Your Adult Children—Companion Study Guide
SANITY Support Group Workbook & Leader Guide
6-STEPS TO SANITY AND 12-WEEKS TO FREEDOM
   Copyright © 2014 by Allison Bottke
   Published by Allison Bottke LLC
   Fort Worth, TX 76137
   AllisonBottke.com
   SettingBoundariesBooks.com

Library of Congress Cataloging-in-Publication Data
Bottke, Allison.
6-STEPS TO SANITY AND 12-WEEKS TO FREEDOM / Allison Bottke

   First printing............May 2008
   Second Printing ....December 2008
   Third Printing ....September 2012
   Fourth Printing (V4) ....August 2014 (First combined version of Workbook & Leader Guide)

Allison Bottke LLC
Setting Boundaries Books
7420 N. Beach Street, Suite 212-73
Fort Worth, TX 76137

NOTE: Please check website "Contact" page to verify mailing address.

   Email
   Allison@AllisonBottke.com

   Web Sites
   AllisonBottke.com
   SettingBoundariesBooks.com

This publication is designed to provide accurate and authoritative information with regard to the subject matter covered. It is sold with the understanding that the author and publisher are not engaged in rendering legal, counseling, or other professional advice. If legal advice or other expert professional assistance is required, the services of a competent professional person should be sought.
~ *Adapted from the Declaration of Principles jointly adopted by a Committee of the American Bar Association and a Committee of Publishers and Associations.*

ISBN-13: 978-0692273951
ISBN-10: 0692273956
BISAC Code: FAM033000
Family & Relationships/Parenting/Parents & Adult Children

> *Dedication*
> This 12-week study guide/program is for every
> broken-hearted parent, step-parent, or grandparent
> who is ready to gain SANITY in an insane situation.
> It's never too late to make choices that will change your life.
> *With God all things are possible.*

We've focused for so long on the problems that we've missed asking the right questions and listening to God for the answers.

Although it's high time many of our adult children accept the consequences of their choices, the plain truth is that we must first accept responsibility for our parental choices—past, present, and future.

Our children may never become the responsible adults we want them to be. They may never change. However, we can change ourselves. And we must change how we respond to their choices.

As people of faith, we face a huge challenge: to be changed from the inside out. Real and permanent changes always begin in our own hearts.

We must learn to be firm *and* loving at the same time.

May God give you confidence and strength during this transforming journey to find **SANITY** in all the relationships in your life.

Allison **Bottke**

TABLE OF CONTENTS

"To be frank, officer, my parents never set boundaries."

PROGRAM ORIENTATION

Alison Bottke's

SANITY Support

SIX STEPS TO HOPE AND HEALING

SettingBoundariesBooks.com

WEEK ONE 1

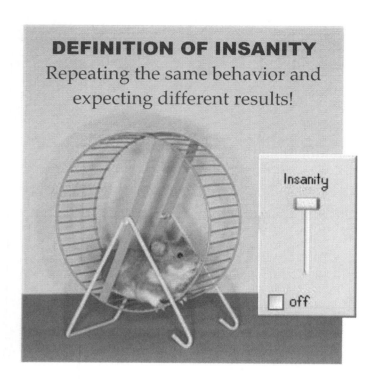

DEFINITION OF INSANITY
Repeating the same behavior and expecting different results!

STOP THE INSANITY NOW!

No matter what the challenging issues may be, if you are living on a gerbil wheel of insanity there are six things you can do *right now* to find **SANITY** in life!

There are six life-changing tools that will help you get off the wheel of insanity, set healthy boundaries, and enjoy the kind of life God wants you to have!

SANITY IS POSSIBLE!

S	STOP	My Usual Responses
A	ASSEMBLE	Supportive People
N	NIP	Excuses in the Bud
I	IMPLEMENT	A Plan of Action
T	TRUST	The Voice of the Spirit
Y	YIELD	Everything to God

Visit us at:
SettingBoundariesBooks.com
Facebook.com/AuthorAllisonBottke

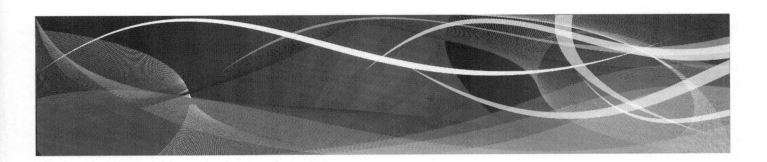

WEEK ONE—PROGRAM ORIENTATION AGENDA

Step One: Open Meeting—Welcome from Group Leader
    Group Leader will use Leader Guide (at back) in tandem with Workbook pages
        - Group Leader Introduction
        - Group Member Introductions
        - Opening Prayer (Group Leader)

Step Two: Let's review pages 8 thru 30 in this Study Guide
    One page at a time...
    Group Leader will use the Group Leader Agenda: Pages 140-142

ARE YOU READY TO TURN AROUND?

Setting healthy boundaries in our relationships isn't about our kids, spouses, parents, siblings, or difficult people.

It's not about what they do or don't do. It's not about changing them.

It's about *our* ability to understand and establish healthy boundaries regarding *our own choices*, and then sticking with them. It's about *us* being consistent with *our* responses when our boundaries are violated. *It's about changing ourselves*.

We cannot change other people. We can change only ourselves—how we choose to respond to our loved ones' behavior, good or bad. And you know what? *It's never too late to change*—because **God Allows U-Turns!**

Learning to respond in a firm *and* loving way isn't easy. Emotional pain and anger often clouds our judgment and diminishes our strength. If our own efforts have failed us, then our success depends on having God's help.

The SANITY principles can work for any parent willing to make the changes needed for stronger and healthier relationships with their adult children. These principles, which form the acronym SANITY, are the foundation of all the books in the *Setting Boundaries®* series.

Are you ready to set healthy boundaries and take back your life? My prayer is that by using the principles of SANITY your life will change. That you'll find hope and healing in these pages, and in the warm embrace of a God who loves you—<u>and</u> your adult children.

God bless you on the journey you are about to take!

~ Allison

THE FAITH COMPONENT OF SETTING BOUNDARIES WITH YOUR ADULT CHILDREN

Throughout the pages of *Setting Boundaries® with Your Adult Children*, you see my perspective as a Christian parent in pain. However, I invite readers of all faiths to learn how to set healthy boundaries. I believe all parents can develop sane relationships with their adult children—even with those whose lives seem to be never-ending stories of drama, chaos and crisis.

A critical part of any enduring solution will be found in a firm trust in God along the way. Long ago, I discovered that God knows our pain. One can scarcely read the gospel account of the prodigal son without deep compassion for the pained father who had to let his son go and longed for his return.

God knows our hearts are breaking. He knows that our adult children and their problems have become ever-present wounds, refusing to heal. When it seems there is no solution to the problem, we need to start looking in the right place. God has the answer. We can have hope because He is present and wants to make us whole, healing our wounds.

As this program takes you on a journey toward healing, I pray that you will also develop a closer relationship with your Higher Power—with God as you know Him to be. When you apply the "Y" step in SANITY, and *Yield Everything to God*, you will be amazed at the incredible freedom you will discover!

Yielding Everything to God *is the only way to peace. The day we came to our wit's end and gave our son 100 percent to the Lord was the day a miracle occurred. We were flooded with His peace, the kind that cannot be explained. We knew then why Jesus came: not only to save our souls but to give us His power to live through anything. Since that time, we have had to do that again and surrender our grandchildren. His grace is sufficient for all things. He is all we need.*

~ Judy Hampton, Author

6-Steps to SANITY
and 12-Weeks to Freedom

**As you begin your journey
on the road to SANITY**

YOU'LL DISCOVER...

- The difference between positively helping and negatively enabling.
- Why we negatively enable and why we must stop.
- The power of love and forgiveness.
- Love is *not* spelled **M-O-N-E-Y**.
- Sometimes it's a good thing to say *no*.
- Saying no does *not* make us bad parents or grandparents.
- How to identify and stop our own negative behaviors.
- How to identify whose chaos and crisis it really is.
- How to separate our own lives from the lives of our adult children.
- How to develop a Plan-of-Action that works.
- The power of considering the consequences.
- How to be strong *and* loving during turbulent times.
- How to view trials and tribulations as stepping stones to great things.
- Why it's vital to belong to a SANITY Support group.
- The importance of trusting the still, small voice of the Holy Spirit.
- The value of yielding everything to God.
- How to love our adult children enough to let them go.
- The joy of what it feels like to *live our own lives*.

SANITY MAKES A COMEBACK!

SANITY SUPPORT MEETING GUIDELINES

These guidelines are intended to enhance the support-group experience and make everyone a more effective Group Member (GM). They are "proven suggestions" based on what groups have found to be the best way to make interaction effective. Ideas shared within the group are intended as support, encouragement, and insight as you walk through challenging times. The author of the *Setting Boundaries*® book series and the Group Leader (GL) facilitator, want to provide a safe, healthy, and non-judgmental environment where you can find hope, healing, and SANITY. However, this group does not seek to take the place of professional or legal counseling.

1. **Materials:** Every GL and GM must have their own copies of the book *Setting Boundaries® with Your Adult Children* and this *SANITY Support Study Guide*. Any photocopying or other reproduction of original materials is not permitted, and is a violation of copyright law. (Except where noted otherwise, such as in forms, flyers, and handouts.)

2. **Agenda**: Meetings will follow the established **WEEKLY AGENDA** (pg. 25), with a goal to begin and end promptly at the scheduled time. Every meeting will begin and end in prayer, and include an audible reading of the **SANITY SUPPORT CREED** (pg. 17) by a GM volunteer.

3. **Phones/Texting**: Cell phones should be turned off or put on vibrate. If you must take a call or respond to a text message, please leave the room so other members are not distracted. Photos are prohibited, as are any forms of audio/visual recording via phone or other electronic devices.

4. **Attendance:** Please be prompt. This allows everyone to start together on the same page. If at all possible, plan to attend all twelve sessions, even if you think some topics do not apply or will not benefit you. Valuable insight can be gained from all the topics, which may prove useful in unforeseen circumstances. Meetings are closed to adult children, guests, and visitors. **NOTE**: In order to develop a strong and trusting group relationship dynamic, new GM's should not be added after week two.

5. **Sharing:** Group Members may share as much or as little about themselves as they desire. Sharing with the group is not mandatory, but we encourage you to do so, because everyone will benefit. Sharing *will greatly help you* in your journey. (See Guidelines 6, 7, 8, & 9 for more about sharing.)

6. Sensitivity: Please be sensitive to the needs of others in the group. Do not dominate the conversation or talk in small groups while another person is sharing. The group needs to give everyone time to talk, and to respect what is being shared, even if you don't agree. Limit personal sharing to 3-5 minutes.

7. Advice and Judgment (aka: Crosstalk): Group Members may be at different stages in the process of setting healthy boundaries and finding SANITY. Everyone is encouraged to lend a comforting ear to listen, a soft shoulder on which to cry, a shared prayer to uplift, and a willingness to be non-judgmental. Group Members are discouraged from telling another GM how to act or think, questioning or interrupting someone who is sharing, or offering specific advice or recommendations. This applies also to the GL unless he or she is a Licensed Counselor and is able to offer *generalized* therapeutic advice based on professional experience.

8. Venting: Many of us who need healthy boundaries in our relationships with our adult children have a bad habit that needs to be avoided—the habit of focusing on the drama, chaos, and crisis that our adult children are experiencing, yet neglecting to expose *how we are responding* to it. Finding SANITY isn't about focusing on the issues our adult children have or the choices they may or may not be making. It's about *how we are responding* to their issues, and the choices *we* may or may not be making. Therefore, please keep the details of their issues and poor choices to a minimum. **Vent about *yourself* in the dynamic—*not* just about your kids.**

This will be quite challenging for many of us, especially as we process feelings of anger, blame, fear, and guilt. Some of us have never talked about these feelings, and when we begin to vent, we're like an exploding pressure cooker—spilling emotions everywhere. It's okay to own and share these varied emotions. In many cases, these emotions are part of the hurt we are striving to heal, which often stands in the way of our finding SANITY. But lamenting over what our kids are doing (or not doing) won't help *us* change. Everyone is encouraged to take ownership of *their portion* of the relationship dynamic as we seek personal growth and SANITY. **NOTE:** Group Leaders (not fellow GM's) are encouraged to gently shift the venting focus if necessary.

9. Confidentiality: What happens in a SANITY Support meeting stays within the confines of a SANITY Support meeting. This is a place of comfort, safety, and personal and spiritual growth. Anything shared in the group must not be repeated to people outside the group. These boundaries of discretion must be maintained to achieve an atmosphere of trust, respect, and concern for one another and promote healing. Our sessions need to reflect a safe environment.

10. Accountability: God works in mysterious ways, and it's no accident you are here. Finding SANITY is all about our willingness to change and be held accountable. Are we ready to stop looking primarily at the challenging lives of our adult children and focus on our own? Are we ready to make choices that will change the story of our life?

> *Time will tell.*

COLD WAR COMBATANTS: During the next twelve weeks, we will identify the two combatants in a dysfunctional boundary battle, better understand each side's needs, and learn how to end the cold war. *It's time to stop the insanity.* Finding SANITY is about neutralizing the conflict and finding peace. It's all about learning how to respond with firmness *and* love.

1. OUR ADULT CHILDREN: Let's face it, when we are dealing with "challenging" adult children, many of them have no concept of healthy boundaries as they pertain to parents or other authority figures. They may be addicted to drugs or alcohol. Sex or pornography is often an issue. Gambling, even video games, can be a destructive force. To support their addictions, some are involved in illegal activity, perhaps in and out of jail more than once. They may be abusive or complacent, with little or no desire to work or even get an education that would qualify them for work. Many have a distorted sense of entitlement, including some who are going to college or trade school as a result of our financial support. Some have grown accustomed to living beyond their means, expecting others to bail them out when they face a financial crisis. If they live with us, they often treat our home like a hotel, checking in and out according to whatever crisis exists at the time. They may bring their spouse or "significant other" to live with them, and many of them expect us to raise their children. Varying degrees of physical, emotional, social, and psychological handicaps exist, often leaving them in dire straits, needing to make better choices.

2. OURSELVES: Some of us have forgotten how important it is to take care of our own personal health and growth. Many of us have spent years coming to the rescue of our adult children. We have provided for, taken care of, bailed out, made excuses for, cried over, prayed for, and have focused an unhealthy amount of time and attention on our adult children. In the process, we have neglected our own mental, emotional, spiritual, physical, and financial health. Other family members have suffered as well, as our challenging adult children have taken so much of our energy. As tempers flare and situations spiral out of control, some of our marriages fall apart. After years of living without boundaries, neglecting our own needs for the sake of our adult children, we are barely able to survive. In dire straits, we've reached the end of our rope, and we really need to make better—and different—choices.

.

IT'S TIME TO CHANGE!

Are you ready to gain control of your life and what happens in your home?
Congratulations! You've taken the first step by reading this far.
Now, get ready for the journey that can change your life.

Get ready to find **SANITY!**

GOD WILL LEAD US IN THE DIRECTION HE WANTS US TO GO
Get ready to live your life!

After years of worrying, rescuing, and negatively enabling our adult children, we have no idea what it feels like to walk in peace.

We don't know what God wants from us or for us. We aren't sure what can be accomplished in our own lives. In fact, we've been misled to believe it's selfish to even consider living our own lives. Many of our past goals and heartfelt dreams have died.
How sad.
This isn't how God wants us to live.

We may feel at the end of the road, or totally exhausted from praying for our adult children. But take a deep breath, **SANITY** is on the way!

For the next 12-weeks,
we'll work hard to break the habit of ignoring ourselves—of putting our own health and happiness on the back burner while rescuing our adult children.

For the next 12-weeks,
we'll learn more about Who is rescuing us.

And we're going to learn
that we are worth rescuing!

Your Prescription to Hope and Healing

SettingBoundariesBooks.com

There will be things in life beyond your control—things you cannot change, and the best way to cope with the stress of those things is to depend on God and put your trust in Him. Pray for the understanding and courage you need to change the things you *can* control—the things God wants you to control in order to fulfill His purpose for your life. *God has a plan for you—and for your adult children!*

If you or someone you know has struggled with alcohol or drug addiction you may be familiar with this prayer below. The *Serenity Prayer* is the common name for an originally untitled prayer by the theologian Reinhold Niebuhr, and has been adopted by Alcoholics Anonymous, other twelve-step programs, and many independent recovery programs.

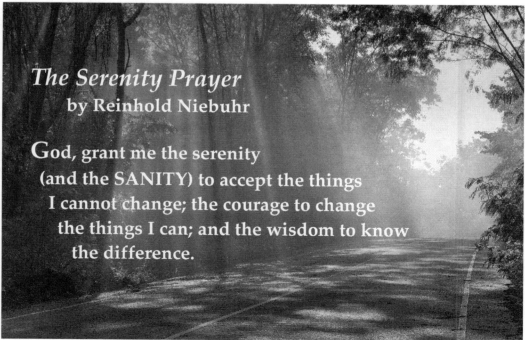

The Serenity Prayer
by Reinhold Niebuhr

God, grant me the serenity
(and the SANITY) to accept the things
I cannot change; the courage to change
the things I can; and the wisdom to know
the difference.

It's a much longer prayer, but this is the part that is most often quoted. And because it speaks to our need to change, we will also adopt this powerful prayer (with one slight addition) as a way to open our weekly meetings.

Our Mission

To bring hope, healing and freedom to parents, step-parents, and grandparents who are struggling with issues concerning challenging relationships with adult children who are often in crisis.

Our Goal

To help parents develop a Plan-of-Action that brings hope, healing and freedom into their lives, and hopefully by example, into the lives of their adult children as well.

Our Prayer

That parents around the world will use the principles of SANITY to change their lives for the better, growing closer to God—and hopefully to their adult children as well.

SANITY SUPPORT CREED

To be read aloud every week by a Group Member volunteer.
(substitute him/her as needed.)

I cannot change the life of my adult child, no matter how much I would like to. However, I can change myself and the choices I make. Today I will make choices based on love, not anger. I will set healthy boundaries with my adult child by choosing to follow the **6-Steps to SANITY**. What my adult child does with his life is his choice. I will no longer accept responsibility for his choices. I will be firm *and* loving at the same time. I will stop thinking it is selfish to focus on my own health and well-being. I will love my adult child—and myself—enough to let go of my own negative habits. I understand pain is often necessary for God to do His best work, and I choose to let God do a good work in me—and in the life of my adult child.

I will gain SANITY and take back my life!

True Stories of Hope and Healing
Compiled and edited by Allison Bottke,
and written by hundreds of authors from around the world.

From Allison's Heart

I understand your pain and confusion. I don't have all the answers. I wish I did. When I wrote *Setting Boundaries® with Your Adult Children*, my son was serving time in a state prison. My heart ached for him. I loved Chris so much and wanted him to live a productive and happy life. I couldn't imagine what it was like for him to be in bondage on so many levels.

But he was an adult capable of making his own choices. So was I. Unfortunately, the choices I made over the years were not always wise, especially when it came to how I responded to the choices my son was making.

However, it's never too late to change direction. The *God Allows U-Turns* books form an entire outreach built on that fact. It's never too late to change the story of our lives.

One of the first steps I took in setting healthy boundaries with my son was to identify the ways I had contributed to the problem. *Ouch.* Believe me, this wasn't an easy exercise—but it was a necessary first step— followed by a willingness to STOP blaming myself for everything. Guilt was my middle name, can you relate?

My life began to change after I recognized what needed to change in me—*not* when my son began to change.

Gaining SANITY isn't a sudden event. It's a process, and sometimes it's painful. It isn't easy to face our own personal issues and see where we've been too flexible, too tolerant, or unwilling to make the tough choices needed.

And that's one of the reasons the reading assignments throughout this course are critical, particularly the list of twenty questions on pages 30–31 in the book. *Don't sugar-coat your responses to these questions.*

If my words sound harsh, please know that it's because I care. I've been there, right where you are, and there's no way to avoid the harsh reality. I love my son, and it always hurts to see him hurt, yet I'm learning that pain is often necessary for God to do some of His greatest work.

Sometimes, when circumstances have gone so far wrong—when the scales of life have tipped so far off—only drastic measures will bring life back into balance. I believe you can find that balance here—in this SANITY Support Group environment.

My prayer is for you to have a life filled with peace, joy, and hope. And as you begin to live your life with healthy boundaries and SANITY, perhaps your adult children will find peace and joy in their own lives.

Trust that God has a plan and a purpose for your life.

God believes in you, I believe in you, and now it's time to believe in yourself.

Allison Bottke

Washington, December 1848

Dear Johnston:

Your request for eighty dollars, I do not think it best to comply with now. At the various times when I have helped you a little, you have said to me, "We can get along very well now," but in a very short time I find you in the same difficulty again. Now this can only happen by some defect in your conduct. What that defect is, I think I know. You are not lazy, and still you are an idler. I doubt whether since I saw you, you have done a good whole day's work, in any one day. You do not very much dislike to work, and still you do not work much, merely because it does not seem to you that you could get much for it. This habit of uselessly wasting time, is the whole difficulty; and it is vastly important to you, and still more so to your children, that you should break this habit. It is more important to them, because they have longer to live, and can keep out of an idle habit before they are in it easier than they can get out after they are in.

You are now in need of some ready money; and what I propose is, that you shall go to work, "tooth and nail," for somebody who will give you money for it. Let father and your boys take charge of things at home—prepare for a crop, and make the crop; and you go to work for the best money wages, or in discharge of any debt you owe, that you can get. And to secure you a fair reward for your labor, I now promise you that for every dollar you will, between this and the first of next May, get for your own labor either in money or in your own indebtedness, I will then give you one other dollar. By this, if you hire yourself at ten dollars a month, from me you will get ten more, making twenty dollars a month for your work. In this, I do not mean you shall go off to St. Louis, or the lead mines, or the gold mines, in California, but I mean for you to go at it for the best wages you can get close to home, in Coles County. Now if you will do this, you will soon be out of debt, and what is better, you will have a habit that will keep you from getting in debt again. But if I should now clear you out, next year you will be just as deep in as ever.

You say you would almost give your place in Heaven for $70 or $80. Then you value your place in Heaven very cheaply, for I am sure you can with the offer I make you get the seventy or eighty dollars for four or five months' work. You say if I furnish you the money you will deed me the land, and if you don't pay the money back, you will deliver possession—Nonsense! If you can't now live with the land, how will you then live without it? You have always been kind to me, and I do not now mean to be unkind to you. On the contrary, if you will but follow my advice, you will find it worth more than eight times eighty dollars to you.

Affectionately your brother,

A. LINCOLN

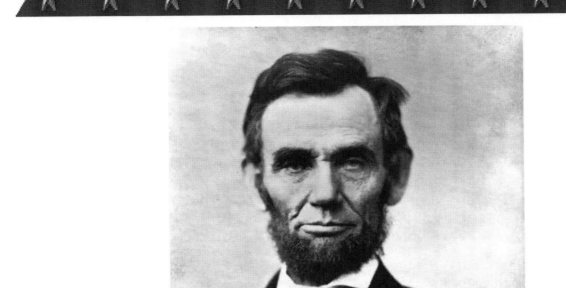

Abraham Lincoln
February 12, 1809—April 15, 1865

16th President of USA
March 4, 1861—April 15, 1865

Work is not child abuse.
~ Dave Ramsey

A BOOK REVIEW BY ANGELA HUNT

Once upon a time, in a country not so far away, children grew up, left home for college, and got married. By age 25 or so they were ensconced in families of their own, and the cycle began all over again...

That's not happening any more. I left home at 18 and married at 22 (the very DAY after my college graduation), but I don't see anything close to that happening with my children or most of the children of my friends. I'm not sure why society has shifted, but it has, and parents are often at a loss when dealing with these twenty-something children who are not ready (or willing) to be on their own and not quite children, either.

My good friend Allison Bottke has written a book, *Setting Boundaries with Your Adult Children*, that may be a lifesaver for you or someone you know. Allison did tons of research, speaking with parents and other authorities about how we can love our children without enabling them. About how we can honor God in our child-rearing efforts at an age when child-rearing is usually long finished.

If you have a challenging adult child, you need to read this book. Seriously.

I have seen so many parents nearly bankrupt themselves and completely drain themselves emotionally because these ought-to-be-grown children can't seem to stand on their own two feet. We seem to be very good at making excuses for them, and not so good at setting boundaries . . . (see the "N" step in SANITY.)

(One day on *Good Morning America*, I watched a mother defend her "wonderful" son who had hired hit men to kill his parents. Parental love is a powerful thing, but boy, can it be blind...)

Allison lists 6-Steps to SANITY, and then explores them.

I highly recommend this book.

~ **Angela Hunt**, Bestselling Author, *The Note, Tale of Three Trees*, and more.

AngelaHuntBooks.com

Setting Boundaries with Your Adult Children will launch a brand new beginning in your life. You may feel you are in a desert place right now as you struggle with a parenting crisis, but be alert! There's a stream in the wasteland—and you can begin making hope-filled choices that will forever change your future for the better.

~ Carol Kent, Speaker and Author

No one knows better the pain of dealing with adult children who have lost their way better than the parents of those without boundaries. Sometimes it feels as though the setting of these boundaries is more difficult than living with the anxiety, stress, and heartache, but that's not so. Allison Bottke, writing through her own hurt and experience, has compiled a masterpiece of advice. She doesn't just tell you or show you how it's done. She walks along beside you.

~ Eva Marie Everson, Author and Speaker

My adult child has been dependent on me for years. Isn't it too late to set (name) free now? How will (name) survive on his/her own?

Nothing is impossible with God! It's never too late to encourage healthy independence in the lives of our adult children. It's surprising how quickly some kids can grow up when given the opportunity. We must bring a stop to unhealthy dependency.

Okay...I'm not quite sure how I'm going to do this, but I'm willing to try. I've joined a SANITY Support Group, and I'm going to try and look at the part I've played in this dysfunctional dynamic over the years and figure out ways I can change. What should I do first?

Good for you! I think the best "first thing" you can do is ask God to give you wisdom and discernment, and then repeat the SANITY Support CREED over and over until it becomes a part of your conscious memory. Congrats on taking this step forward!

WEEKLY AGENDA
This timeframe format will be used every week

<u>Meeting Length</u>: 90-minutes (or 2-hr. option—see note below)

<u>Step One</u>—**5 minutes:** Open Meeting
 ~ Cell phones off, get quiet and focused
 ~ Group Reading—**Serenity Prayer** (Page 16)
 ~ One Group Member Reads the **SANITY CREED** (Page 17)

<u>Step Two</u>—**30 minutes:** Group Discussion
 Review Previous Week Primary Action Items
 (As identified in **Step Four** of previous week.)

<u>Step Three</u>—**40 minutes:** Group Discussion
 Fill-in-the-Blank Homework
 (To be accomplished *before* this weekly session.)

<u>Step Four</u>—**10 minutes:** Identify Your Primary Action Item(s)
 (Your main goal: *This week I am going to...*)

<u>IF THERE IS TIME</u>: Review the "Other Important Pages" before moving on to Step Five and Step Six.

<u>Step Five</u>—**3 minutes:** What's in Store for Next Week
 ~ Review book pages to read before next meeting
 ~ Confirm date and time for next meeting

<u>Step Six</u>—**2 minutes:** Closing Prayer
 ~ Included at the end of each weekly session

90-minute mark: Adjourn Meeting

Option: Group may elect to extend session an additional 30-minutes for fellowship, refreshments, and/or individual prayer. Or, to begin earlier with a potluck dinner or light refreshments.

God has a plan for your life!

154   Setting Boundaries with Food

Three Life-Changing Questions

I ask three questions at the start of my SANITY Support workshops for struggling parents who are caught in the bondage of dysfunctional relationships with adult children. Most often, the response I get is a deer-in-the-headlights stare.

1. What would you do with your life if you weren't so wrapped up in the ongoing drama, chaos, and crisis that surrounds your life with your adult child—if you weren't dealing with the never-ending sagas of their unemployment, addictions, financial challenges, and poor choices?

2. What would you do with the time if you stopped being responsible for the consequences of their choices?

3. What would you do with the money if you stopped funding their lives and stopped trying to solve their problems with your checkbook?

By the time they seek SANITY Support, many of these precious souls have spent countless hours—and often countless dollars as well—trying to help their adult kids. In so doing, they've all but lost track of who they are as separate individuals—children of an almighty God.

But something amazing happens when we begin to set healthy boundaries in our lives, when we put God first, when we begin to say no to the roadblocks in our path, when we begin to understand what it means to walk in our own calling and purpose, and when we begin to find sanity, fully commit ourselves to God, and trust that He is in control. We begin to experience life.

> Trust in the LORD and do good;
> dwell in the land and enjoy safe pasture.
> Take delight in the LORD,
> and he will give you the desires of your heart.
> Commit your way to the LORD;
> trust in him and he will do this:
> He will make your righteous reward shine like the dawn,
> your vindication like the noonday sun (Psalm 37:3-6 NIV).

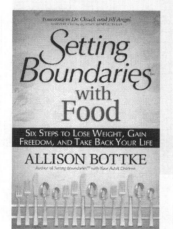

Foreword by *Dr. Chuck and Jill Angel*

Setting
Boundaries
with
Food

SIX STEPS TO LOSE WEIGHT, GAIN
FREEDOM, AND TAKE BACK YOUR LIFE

ALLISON BOTTKE

Author of *Setting Boundaries with Your Adult Children*

Page 154

Setting
Boundaries
With
Food

Get ready to begin experiencing YOUR LIFE!

Are you ready?

Are you serious about setting healthy boundaries and finding SANITY?

Do you really want to change your life? If so, you're in the right place! The goal for next week is to hit the ground running, to jump into the pool's deep end and see if you're ready to swim. *Are you?* There's a lot of reading to do before the next session. There's a lot of homework to complete.

There's also the possibility that this could be the start of a new life. So I ask you again....are you ready?

SANITY Support
Group Member Covenant Agreement

I, _____ stand in agreement with my fellow SANITY Support group members to do the following:

1. Complete the reading and writing assignments each week before the group session.
2. Pray regularly for my adult child, fellow group members, group leader, and for myself.
3. Strive to be on time for every session.
4. Make sure my cell phone is off before we begin. Be fully present in each session.
5. Participate in all group sessions unless urgent circumstances beyond my control prevent my attendance. When unable to attend, I will make up the session in order to stay on track.
6. Participate openly and honestly in the group sessions.
7. Keep confidential everything shared by others in the group.
8. Be sensitive to the needs of the entire group and not dominate the conversation.
9. Be patient with my fellow group members as God works in us all to make us what He wants us to be. I will trust God to convict me (and others) of His will. I will not try to manipulate or pressure others to do what I think is best. I will simply bear witness of what I sense God may be saying to us and watch to see how the Holy Spirit uses that witness.
10. Pray at least weekly for my pastor and my church (if I don't belong to a church, I will pray about this and ask God to open doors.) Pray also for Allison Bottke as she continues to follow God's call to share the life-changing message of setting healthy boundaries and finding SANITY.

Signed: _____ Date: _____

Today's Date: _____

This is how I feel: _____

_____

This is what I need/want: _____

Week One

Today's Date: _____

This is how I feel: _____

_____

This is what I received: _____

_____

Week Twelve

BEFORE NEXT WEEK'S MEETING

SPECIAL REMINDER: This is the most homework you'll ever have in one week.

- **Read Foreword & Why I Wrote this Book** (Book Pages 9-24)
- **Read Part One — The Parent as Enabler** (Book Pages 25-95)
    - Chapter 1 — But I'm Only Trying to Help
    - Chapter 2 — Why We Enable, and Why We Must Stop
    - Chapter 3 — Get Smart and Take Action
    - Chapter 4 — But Deep Down He's Really a Good Kid
    - Chapter 5 — The Power of Love and Forgiveness
- **Complete Week Two** writing assignments in this workbook *before next session*

Week One: CLOSING PRAYER

Thank You, Lord, that there is power in Your Name. Thank You for bringing me to this place where I can begin to make different choices that will change my life. I know I've made mistakes. Help me, Lord, to cast off the feelings of guilt and blame that have weighed heavily on my heart. I can't do this alone. Give me courage and faith to continue this journey of setting new boundaries in my life. I proclaim that You, Jesus, are Lord over my life and over everything that happens to me — and to my adult child. You have a purpose for my life and for my child's life. Help me live my life as You would have me live it, and help my child learn how to accept responsibility for his/her life. ~Amen

THE PARENT AS ENABLER

Alison Bottke's
SANITY Support
SIX STEPS TO HOPE AND HEALING
SettingBoundariesBooks.com

WEEK TWO 2

WEEK TWO—THE PARENT AS ENABLER

Setting Boundaries with Your Adult Children
Part One: The Parent as Enabler (Pages 1-95)

Step One: Open Meeting—5 minutes
1. Cell phones off, take a moment to get quiet and focused
2. Group Reading—The Serenity-SANITY Prayer (Page 16)
3. One Group Member Reads the SANITY Creed (Page 17)

Step Two: Group Discussion—30 min.—How was your week?

Step Three: Group Discussion Points—40 min. (Fill-in-the-blank homework.)

1. We need a better understanding of the difference between **HELPING** and **ENABLING**.

   a. Helping is doing something for someone that he is _____ capable of doing himself.
   b. Enabling is doing something for someone that he _____ and _____ be doing for himself.
   c. Simply, enabling creates an atmosphere in which our adult children can comfortably _____ their _____ behavior.

2. Are you an enabling parent? Read the list of 20 questions on pages 30-31. How many can you answer with, "Yes?"

   ☐ 1-5 ☐ 6-10
   ☐ 11-15 ☐ 16-20

3. Why do we enable in the first place? Read the list on page 44. Do any of these apply to you?

      ☐ Yes   ☐ No   ☐ Uncertain

4. Change Can be Freeing or Frightening. (Page 66)
What will we do when we _____ living our adult children's lives for them? We will _____ living our own!

Which of the Ten Steps on pages 66-67 do you think will be the most helpful?

_____

_____

5. Is your adult child really, "a good kid deep down inside?" Take the painful exercise and answer "yes" or "no" the 20 questions on pages 76 and 77.

TOTAL NUMBER: Yes = _____   No = _____

Was this exercise difficult? If so, why?

_____

_____

_____

6. In taking the necessary steps to stop enabling my son and to set healthy boundaries, I found it necessary to look at five areas of **FORGIVENESS**. (Page 86)

Do any of these five areas on page 86 apply to you?
☐ Yes ☐ No ☐ Uncertain

Step Four: Identify Your Primary Action Item(s): 10 min.

This week I am going to…

Our desire as parents is to respond to our children with love. For many of us, that has been all but impossible to do for quite some time. The anger and animosity run deep. However, the season of change is now upon us.

~ Allison Bottke

If there is time in this session...

If you have time in your group session after **Step Four**, review the additional pages included in this section.

If you are out of time, please move on to **Step Five** and to the *Closing Prayer* in **Step Six**. However, make sure to review the important information (listed below) on your own.

Additional Information:
- A New Way to Pray for Your Adult Children—page 35
- One Minute Prayers for Your Adult Children—page 35
- Ways We Enable—page 36
- An Ex-Enabler Speaks Out—page 36
- Allison's Top Ten Suggestions for Breaking the Enabling Cycle—page 37
- How to Stay Connected—page 38
- The Will of God —page 39

CLOSING STEPS FIVE & SIX: PAGE 40

A New Way to Pray for Your Adult Children

How You Can Pray When You Are Holding the Rope For Your Loved One
by Sharon Hill, Founder of *OnCall Prayer* ™

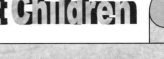

Start by reading Acts 9:20-25. Ask God to help change your heart first and then for the strength to pray lovingly for your adult child while also setting healthy boundaries in firm and loving ways.

Intentionally ask God for these five specific acts concerning your adult child.

> **Pray ...** *Dear Lord,*
> 1. ...**make** the scales fall away from the eyes of my child. (Acts 9:18-19)
> 2. ...**give** my child the desire to TOTALLY SURRENDER to You. (Joshua 22:5)
> 3. ...**replace** my child's heart of stone with a new heart. (Ezekiel 36:26-27)
> 4. ...**instill** a hunger for God's presence in the life of my child. (Deuteronomy 4:29-31)
> 5. ...**enable** my child to become a mighty man/woman of God! (Psalm 112:1-2)

We must begin to change the way we pray for our adult children. Our prayers must become more *intentional*.

ALLISON BOTTKE
Bestselling author of *Setting Boundaries® with Your Adult Children*

One-Minute
PRAYERS™
for your
Adult Children

WAYS WE ENABLE OUR ADULT CHILDREN

- Being "The Bank of Mom and Dad," or "The Bank of Grandma and Grandpa."

- Loaning money that is never repaid, buying what our children can't afford and don't really need.

- Continually coming to their rescue so they don't feel the pain—the consequences—of their actions and choices.

- Accepting excuses we know are excuses—and in some instances are blatant lies. (Excuses are most often justification for unacceptable behavior.)

- Blaming ourselves for all (or many of) their problems.

An Ex-Enabler Speaks Out (Actual email from a reader.)

A friend gave me your book and told me how it changed her life. I was having problems with my then sixteen-year-old son. I read the book and told her I thought it was great, but my problems were not *"that bad"* and I could handle them. About a year later, I could not ignore the problems anymore and finally had to admit that I could not control my son. He ended up in intensive care for two weeks after "dying" twice on the table due to drugs. He was released from the hospital and I thanked God for a second chance—certain everything was going to be perfect now. Hmmm...yeah, not really.

Next thing I know he's swinging golf clubs at his father and me, stealing everything to get money for drugs and alcohol, and threatening to have me arrested. My friend told me to read your book again. I did—and I feel like a new person, with newfound strength. I finally looked in the mirror at myself and realized I cannot change my son. I can only change my reactions.

My son is on a downward spiral. He no longer lives in our house, and I have not given him any money since we asked him to leave. I love him dearly, but my husband and daughter are worth more than that. I am worth more than that. I can only pray and love him and wait for him to accept our love, but more importantly, God's love. It will happen, and when it does, he will have an amazing testimony like in Jeremiah 29:11: "For I know the plans I have for you," declares the Lord, "plans to prosper you and not to harm you, plans to give you hope and a future."

Without your book, without God's love and strength and without my very strong friend, I am convinced that I would not be here today. I fear that I would not be alive. I am proud to say that I am no longer my son's enabler. I am a wife, a mother, and a very proud Christian.

In return, I have handed out your book to at least five different friends.

Thank you...thank you...thank you!!!

~ LB

ALLISON'S TOP-TEN SUGGESTIONS FOR BREAKING THE ENABLING CYCLE

1. You shall take care of your own spiritual, mental, physical, emotional, and financial health.

2. You shall remember to express love and attention to your spouse and other family members and friends in addition to your troubled adult child.

3. You shall not accept excuses.

4. You shall understand that a clear definition of right and wrong is imperative for a disciplined society. There is no room for gray. Don't make excuses for what you believe.

5. You shall make fact-based judgments without excuse and feel okay doing so.

6. You shall uphold standards of behavior that protect your morals, values, and integrity.

7. You shall give your adult child unconditional love and supportive encouragement without meddling and without money.

8. You shall listen to music and read books that will focus your mind on God.

9. You shall celebrate life and love as often as possible, even in times of trouble.

10. You shall consistently practice the **6-Steps to SANITY** as outlined in ***Setting Boundaries with Your Adult Children.***

HOW TO STAY CONNECTED

Join our growing online community of people who have experienced the Six Steps to SANITY

SANITY SUPPORT BLOG
SettingBoundariesBooks.com/blog

SETTING BOUNDARIES WEBSITE
SettingBoundariesBooks.com

FACEBOOK—SANITY SUPPORT for TEENS
Facebook.com/SanitySupportForYoungWomen

FACEBOOK—SETTING BOUNDARIES BOOKS
Facebook.com/AuthorAllisonBottke

TWITTER
@AllisonBottke

ALLISON'S WEBSITE
AllisonBottke.com

GOOGLE +
Allison@AllisonBottke.com

E-MAIL
Allison@AllisonBottke.com

LINKEDIN
www.linkedin.com/pub/allison-bottke/6/3a5/503

PINTEREST
http://pinterest.com/allisonbottke/

SANITY Support is Available Online 24/7 "Like" us on Facebook Today!

A FACEBOOK Community for SANITY!

Check out our blog!
SettingBoundariesBooks.com/blog

The Will of God will never take you, where the grace of God will not protect you.

SettingBoundariesBooks.com ©

Step Five: What's in Store for Next Week — 3 minutes

- **Read Part Two:** *The Six Steps to SANITY* (Book Pages 97-99)
- If needed, go back and review (or catch-up on) Chapters 1-5
- **Complete Week Three** writing assignments in this workbook *before next session.*
- **Special Announcements:** Group Leader/Members

Step Six: CLOSING PRAYER

Thank You, Lord, for opening my eyes to the ways I have enabled my adult child. Forgive my mistakes and help me see the ways I need to change. Give me wisdom to understand the new parenting journey I must take. Keep all evil thoughts of blame, guilt, and anger away from my heart and mind. Help me fully trust You, no matter what happens. Help me find hope and healing in my journey to be the person You want me to be, and help me live the life You would have me live. And Lord, please teach me how to effectively pray for my child. ~ Amen

SIX STEPS TO SANITY OVERVIEW

Allison Bottke's
SANITY Support
SIX STEPS TO HOPE AND HEALING

SettingBoundariesBooks.com

WEEK THREE 3

S.A.N.I.T.Y.

WEEK THREE—SIX STEPS TO SANITY—OVERVIEW

Setting Boundaries with your Adult children
Part Two: The Six Steps to SANITY (Pages 97-99)

Step One: Open Meeting—5 minutes
1. Cell phones off, take a moment to get quiet and focused
2. Group Reading—The Serenity-SANITY Prayer (Page 16)
3. One Group Member Reads the SANITY Creed (Page 17)

Step Two: Discuss Status of Action Items—30 min. (As identified in Step Four last week.)
How was your week?

Step Three: Group Discussion Points—40 min. (Fill-in-the-blank homework.)

1. What is the possible long term side effect of following the 6-Steps to SANITY?
In time we will begin to regain our SANITY and we will begin to feel a sense of
_____-_____ and _____ despite any crisis.

2. In what situations will SANITY work? We can implement the six steps to help an
adult child grow up who... (Page 98)

    1. _____
    2. _____
    3. _____
    4. _____
    5. _____

3. What negative feelings have we been harboring in the ongoing drama of enabling? (Page 98)

    1. G _____

    2. F _____

    3. A _____

    4. F _____

    5. I _____

4. What are the six steps parents can do to break the cycle of enabling? (Page 99)

    S = _____ your own negative behavior

        (Also, **STOP** blaming yourself and **STOP** the flow of money.)

    A = _____ a support group (or, supportive people)

    N = _____ excuses in the bud

    I = _____ rules and boundaries (develop an Action Plan!)

    T = _____ your instincts (the Voice of the Holy Spirit)

    Y = _____ everything to God ("let go and let God")

Step Four: Identify Your Primary Action Item(s):—10 minutes

SPECIAL GROUP LEADER EXERCISE

Group Leader will distribute slips of paper to each Group Member. Take a moment to read them, pray silently for God to convict your spirit, and then check the boxes that apply. Fold your paper in half and wait for Leader instructions.

Record what you have decided to release…

> **A Reader Speaks Up...**
>
> *I just read Setting Boundaries® with Your Adult Children. It was amazing! Truly God speaks in mysterious ways to get His point across to us. Thank you! I am still reflecting on the book and how best to apply it to my life.*
>
> *Forgiveness is something we mere mortals seem to struggle with constantly. No wonder it is such a big deal to God. The emphasis on forgiveness was subtly woven throughout without being preachy. What a gift!*
>
> *~ LS*

If there is time in this session...

If you have time in your group session after **Step Four**, review the additional pages included in this section.

If you are out of time, please move on to **Step Five** and to the *Closing Prayer* in **Step Six**. However, make sure to review the important information (listed below) on your own.

Additional Information:
- Words from Christopher —page 45
- One Minute Prayers for Your Adult Children—page 46
- No Marshmallows!—page 47

CLOSING STEPS FIVE & SIX: PAGE 48

WORDS FROM CHRISTOPHER

The following text was taken from a letter my son wrote while he was in prison to parents who are in challenging relationships with their adult children.

I guess what it really comes down to is that it's taken me thirty-plus years to come to the conclusion that I alone am responsible for the wrong choices I've made in my life. I spent years blaming my mother, the police, and society. Today, I'm serving time behind bars and I have no one to blame but myself.

I know my mother loves me, and she continues to hope and pray for me. If you have a loved one making wrong choices, don't give up hope—don't stop loving

Christopher & Allison, 2006
Faribault, Minnesota
(Just before lengthy prison sentence.)

them even when they are unlovable. But they need to be set free from your hands so they can learn some lessons on their own. Chances are, you've already given them enough rope to climb more than half way up the mountain. It's time to let them go. Believe me, they will figure out a way to get to the top on their own—one way or another. They won't be stuck mid-way forever.

Set your adult children free to make their own choices and live the consequences. But please, don't dead bolt the door entirely. Some day they will show up and knock and ask forgiveness, and hopefully have some life experience under their belt to realize they need caring people in their life and it's much easier to live with people who genuinely care for you. One day they will admit they didn't know everything—I know I did. It may take longer for some adult children, but I believe the day will come. It came for me. It wasn't easy, and it still isn't.

Parents, don't blame yourself for the actions we take. Many successful, positive, and important people learned the hard way, but they did learn. You need to trust that God can restore a messed-

up life. He's changing mine, and I pray to the Lord every day for the strength and wisdom to make better choices. Like I said, it's not easy. I can't change the past, but I can make better choices in my future. My mom always says that *God Allows U-Turns*. And I say there's no statute of limitations on turning toward Him. No matter what we've done.

Christopher Smith—**March 2008**

2011—Texas

Update: Chris is out of prison, drug-free and walking with the Lord. Our relationship is far from perfect, but at least we're a "work-in-progress" and not a closed book. Here he is working at my book table at a speaking engagement in Texas. *Thank you, Jesus!*

ALLISON BOTTKE
Bestselling author of *Setting Boundaries® with Your Adult Children*

One-Minute
PRAYERS
for your
Adult Children

> *"Keep on asking, and you will receive what you ask for. Keep on seeking, and you will find. Keep on knocking, and the door will be opened to you. For everyone who asks, receives. Everyone who seeks, finds. And to everyone who knocks, the door will be opened."*
> **Matthew 7:7-8 (NLT)**

Over 30 Topics Including...

Addiction, Anger, Change, Consequences, Courage, Depression, Direction, Employment, Enabling, Estrangement, Faith, Fear, Forgiveness, Freedom, God's Love, Grandchildren, Guilt, Healing, Hope, Letting Go, Money, Responsibility, Salvation, Truth, Wisdom, Worship, **and more!**

From One Minute Prayers for Your Adult Children:

The Nourishment of Your Strength

*Even if I go through the deepest darkness,
I will not be afraid, LORD, for you are with me.
Your shepherd's rod and staff protect me.*
PSALM 23:4 GNT

Father God, I've lamented, grieved, and cried out to You about my drug-addicted child. I'm coming to You now to boldly ask for divine mercy and grace. (Name) needs help, but I don't know how to help or even if I should. I'm not a very good judge of what (name) really needs, but You are.

God, give (name) the light of Your love and the nourishment of Your strength. Please help her (him) to beat this life-threatening addiction. In Jesus's mighty name, please deliver my precious daughter (son) from the grip of Satan's influence. Release her (him) from this terrible bondage of addiction. Let (name) know what it feels like to breathe, walk, and exist in Your grace and mercy. Wrap Your loving arms around (name) as she (he) leaves the turbulence behind and steps into the healing flow of Your light and love.

Father God, help me to remember that I cannot change anything in (name's) life but You can change everything. ~ **Amen**

Setting healthy boundaries a'int for marshmallows.
SettingBoundariesBooks.com ©

Step Five: What's in Store for Next Week — 3 minutes

- **Read:** *Step One for Gaining SANITY*
  S = STOP Your Own Negative Behavior (Book Pages 101-110)
- **Complete Week Four** writing assignments in this workbook *before next session*
- **Special Announcements:** Group Leader/Members

Step Six: CLOSING PRAYER

Heavenly Father, you know I'm ready to find SANITY in my life. You know the time has come for me to respond differently to my adult child. You also know that it won't be easy for me. Help me to fully release the negative feelings I have released on paper tonight. Help me in my journey to change myself. Help me respond lovingly. I need your supernatural strength in this journey as I make bold new choices to stop the cycle of enabling. Thank you, Lord, for bringing SANITY into what was once an insane life. I am ready to let You take control and guide me on this path to hope and healing. ~ Amen

S = STOP OUR USUAL RESPONSES

WEEK FOUR 4

WEEK FOUR—*S*—STOP OUR USUAL RESPONSES

Setting Boundaries with Your Adult Children
Step One in Gaining SANITY: STOP Your Usual Responses, STOP Feeling Guilty,
STOP Blaming Yourself, **and** *STOP the Flow of Money* (Pages 101-110)

Step One: Open Meeting—5 minutes
1. Cell phones off, take a moment to get quiet and focused
2. Group Reading—The Serenity-SANITY Prayer (Page 16)
3. One Group Member Reads the SANITY Creed (Page 17)

Step Two: Discuss Status of Action Items—30 min. (As identified in Step Four last week.)
How was your week?

Step Three: Group Discussion Points—40 min. (Fill-in-the-blank homework.)

1. Four critical "Stop Steps" to end the INSANITY: (Page 104)
   STOP repeating negative _____ behavior in all its forms
   STOP _____ our own _____ issues
   STOP being _____ in our _____
   STOP the _____ of _____

2. Change _____ when we _____. (Page 107)

Change will <u>START</u> when we <u>STOP</u> !

If in the course of your new journey, your adult child manages to find his way as well,
this will be an answer to prayer. And although there is no guarantee that your new
choices will be embraced by your adult child, you still need to make
them for your own peace of mind. (Page 109)

---

3. Review some of the reasons on page 106 for why we have made ourselves so available to our adult children. Do any of these reasons apply to you?

☐ Yes   ☐ No   ☐ Uncertain

List your key reasons below.

_____

_____

_____

_____

4. Which of the 12 "Stop Steps" on page 110 do you think will be your most difficult and why? What can you do to help yourself "Stop"?

_____

_____

_____

_____

_____

(Photocopy the list of "Things to Stop Starting Now" at the end of this week's lesson and post it where you'll see it regularly, such as on your refrigerator or bulletin board.)

5. What are your personal life goals and what is the ultimate destination you wish to reach in your lifetime? What is God's plan and purpose for *your* life?

_____

_____

_____

_____

Step Four: Identify Your Primary Action Item(s):—10 minutes

This week I am going to...

CAUTION

When we begin applying the 6-Steps to SANITY, things begin changing. Be aware of your own child's proclivity to violence if he is provoked, and *prepare accordingly.*
~ Allison Bottke

If there is time in this session...

If you have time in your group session after **Step Four**, review the additional pages included in this section.

If you are out of time, please move on to **Step Five** and to the *Closing Prayer* in **Step Six**. However, make sure to review the important information (listed below) on your own.

Additional Information:
- Relax!—page 53
- How We Can Stop—page 54
- Things to STOP, Starting Now—page 55

CLOSING STEPS FIVE & SIX: PAGE 56

HOW WE CAN STOP

1. Make a commitment to change.

2. Follow the 6-Steps to SANITY.

3. Focus on re-prioritizing our relationships.

4. Get help to better understand our own issues.

5. Pray for wisdom and discernment.

WHAT WE NEED TO KNOW

1. God is in control.

2. We have boundary rights and responsibilities.

3. It won't be easy to break bad habits.

4. Change brings consequences, and some may be painful.

5. We are not alone.

WHAT WE NEED TO DO

1. Grow in our relationship with the Father, Son, and Holy Spirit.

2. Stay connected with SANITY Support group members.

3. Develop a written Plan-of-Action.

4. Be committed to change and consistent with choices.

5. Speak the truth in love.

6. Pray! And then, pray some more!

And, *NEVER* give up!

We must STOP stepping in to soften the blow of the circumstances from the choices our adult children are making.

~ Allison Bottke

THINGS TO STOP, STARTING NOW

1. Stop repeating negative enabling behavior in all its forms

2. Stop ignoring my own personal issues

3. Stop being alone in my pain (Join our Facebook community.)

4. Stop the flow of money—now

5. Stop pretending things are going to be fine if I continue as I have been

6. Stop putting off the changes that must be made

7. Stop my own destructive patterns and behaviors

8. Stop feeling guilty

9. Stop demanding that my adult child change

10. Stop making excuses for his or her negative behaviors and/or choices

11. Stop engaging in arguments, debates, or negotiations—no verbal volleyball

12. Stop being a martyr

Something Positive to <u>START</u> Now!

Begin communicating with fellow
SANITY Support group members
and *Setting Boundaries*® readers from
around the world on our 24/7 Facebook community (fan/business) page.

Facebook.com/AuthorAllisonBottke

Step Five: What's in Store for Next Week—3 minutes

- **Read:** *Step Two in Gaining SANITY*
  A = ASSEMBLE a Support Group (Book Pages 111-116)
- **Complete Week Five** writing assignments in this workbook *before next session*
- **Special Announcements:** Group Leader/Members

Step Six: CLOSING PRAYER

Father God, I am ready to STOP. I am ready to STOP all of the negative responses that have kept me from being the parent—and person—You want me to be. I understand that SANITY will begin only when I STOP my negative enabling responses to the choices my adult child makes. I cannot change the choices my adult child makes—but I can change my response to them. Lord, help me find the courage to STOP anything that gets in the way of making the necessary positive changes in my life. Help me STOP going backward and help me move forward with You. Help me to be strong in Your power. ~ Amen

A = ASSEMBLE SUPPORTIVE PEOPLE

Allison Bottke's
SANITY *Support*
SIX STEPS TO HOPE AND HEALING

SettingBoundariesBooks.com

WEEK FIVE 5

WEEK FIVE—4—ASSEMBLE SUPPORTIVE PEOPLE

Setting Boundaries with your Adult Children
Step Two in Gaining SANITY:
    ASSEMBLE a Support Group   (Pages 111-116)

Step One: Open Meeting—5 minutes
1. Cell phones off, take a moment to get quiet and focused
2. Group Reading—The Serenity-SANITY Prayer (Page 16)
3. One Group Member Reads the SANITY Creed (Page 17)

Step Two: Discuss Status of Action Items—30 min. (As identified in Step Four last week.)
How was your week?

Step Three: Group Discussion Points—40 min. (Fill-in-the-blank homework.)

1. Parents in pain need _____, _____,
    _____, and _____ from others who have
    traveled this painful journey and come out on the other side — or from those
    who are currently walking the journey with us. (Page 111)

2. How does the Scripture verse from Ecclesiastes 4:9-12 speak to your heart—and
your circumstances at this point in time?

_____

_____

_____

_____

_____

3. We are now at Week Five in our 12-Week Program, has being in this SANITY Support group helped you to begin any of the following...

- Looking at your circumstances more objectively?

  ☐ Yes ☐ No ☐ Uncertain

- Emotionally distancing yourself from your situation to gain a healthier perspective?

  ☐ Yes ☐ No ☐ Uncertain

- Making clear choices based on facts, not feelings?

  ☐ Yes ☐ No ☐ Uncertain

4. How has prayer and group support helped you begin to find SANITY?

_____

_____

_____

5. How has reading the **SANITY Support CREED** at the start of every weekly session helped you begin to find SANITY?

_____

_____

_____

Step Four: Identify Your Primary Action Item(s):—10 minutes

This week I am going to...

> *Two are better than one, because they have a good return for their work. If one falls down, his friend can help him up...*
> **~ Ecclesiastes 4:9-10**

If there is time in this session...

If you have time in your group session after **Step Four**, review the additional pages included in this section.

If you are out of time, please move on to **Step Five** and to the *Closing Prayer* in **Step Six**. However, make sure to review the important information (listed below) on your own.

Additional Information:
- Get a Jump Start on Your Plan of Action Development—page 61
- Guidelines to Develop Your Plan of Action—pages 62-63
- Forms Available Online Now—page 63
- Stop Putting Your Life on Hold—page 64
- Recommended Resources—page 65

CLOSING STEPS FIVE & SIX: PAGE 66

Let's get a jump start on our
PLAN OF ACTION DEVELOPMENT

Never underestimate the power of a written plan

As We Approach Week Six ...

Feedback from people around the country who have participated in the 6-Steps to SANITY and 12-Weeks to Freedom program indicates that developing a Plan of Action is one of the most challenging aspects of setting healthy boundaries with adult children. We know what we have been doing isn't working. We know what we would like to see happen. We know how we would like to live. But committing this knowledge and goals to paper and defining a timeline to actually implement boundaries is scary. Many of us have been on the gerbil wheel of insanity for so long because we're afraid of what might happen if we decide to be firm and loving and actually make changes. But the time has come to stop living in fear.

STOP the insanity!
Nothing is impossible with God!

Remember the Definition of INSANITY...
Repeating the same behavior and expecting different results!

A Reader Speaks Up...

Sometimes it takes getting the rug pulled out from under your feet to change. I must admit I am learning so much from your book but I am surprised at what I am learning about myself. I can see now why I struggle with setting boundaries, but I am willing to change—I must change!
~BH

GUIDELINES TO DEVELOPING YOUR PLAN OF ACTION
FOUR STEPS TO GETTING JUMP STARTED

In *Setting Boundaries with Your Adult Children*, I advise readers to use six separate spiral notebooks to begin compiling stream-of-consciousness thoughts about their Action Plan components. As time has gone by and readers around the world have participated in this 12-week study, I've found a more effective way to organize and develop your Action Plan.

Please do not underestimate the intrinsic value of this critical step. It may seem like a lot of work, but you are worth it and your relationship with your adult child is worth it. Do not let the enemy sabotage your progress at this point by skipping this step.

Step One: Go to Wal-Mart or any office supply store and purchase:
- One 3-ring binder (1" size)
- One set of 8-Tab Index Inserts
- One pad of lined paper or a package of lined notebook paper, you'll need about 10-pages per section (3-hole punched).

Step Two: Identify the 8-Tab Index Inserts as follows:
1. To Do (Page 162)
2. To Stop (Page 162)
3. Plan Notes (Inc. 6 Areas on page 135 and 6 Components on pages 164-165)
4. Consequences (Pages 177-183)
5. Scripts (Page 163) **Note:** These can also be in a letter format.
6. Resources & Misc. (Page 167)
7. Final Plan
8. My Own Goals

Step Three: Place approximately 10-pages of lined paper in each section.

Step Four: Now, before you start doing any writing, take a deep breath, place your hands on top of the binder, and commit the entire process to God. Harness the power of prayer and God's provision, asking the Lord to give you wisdom, discernment, strength, and peace of mind and heart as you move forward over the next weeks in developing your Action Plan. Pray that your choices and steps to set healthy boundaries and find SANITY will come from a place of love and not anger. It *is* possible to set firm *and* loving boundaries. Your intention is not to punish your adult child, it's to change your own behavior in how you respond to his/her choices.

> We will discuss this topic in greater length in Weeks 7 and 10, but feel free to jump ahead and read Chapter 12 if you are able to do so.

That's it for the initial **Four Steps** to get you jump-started on **Developing Your Plan of Action**. We will begin to seriously discuss this more in Weeks 7 and 10, but feel free to begin writing your stream-of-consciousness thoughts in each section, flipping back and forth between sections as needed. This is where ideas, thoughts, plans, and dreams begin to take root and grow! Resist the urge to edit yourself, just write. If you're married, do this as a couple, perhaps taking turns writing. **NOTE TO COUPLES:** This is where the rubber is going to meet the road for many of you. Discussing a **Plan of Action** and actually *agreeing* on the same **Plan of Action** are sometimes two entirely different things. We're going to talk more about the need for couples to be on the same page if you truly want to find SANITY. But in the mean time, do not let Satan drive a wedge between you if you're finding it hard to agree at this point! Pray for the ability to understand where your loved one is coming from—and for the ability to meet in the middle.

Remember, you didn't get to this place overnight, chances are you will not be able to develop this important document overnight either. Organize the binder and take the time you need to complete each section, *but don't drag your feet.* In Week 7 we will talk about the critical need to establish a timeline to complete your **Plan of Action**; feel free to begin thinking about that now.

> *"Because he loves me," says the Lord, "I will rescue him;*
> *I will protect him, for he acknowledges my name."*
> Psalm 91:14 NIV

Available Now...!!!

SAMPLE FORMS & DOCUMENTS

A critical part of setting healthy boundaries is learning to calmly articulate our goals and to be willing to record them on paper to keep us on track and accountable.
Planning is the key to success.
It's been said that if you aim for nothing, you'll hit it every time.

Sometimes it's difficult to know what to say, to find the words that express our thoughts and feelings in a firm *and* loving way. To help you clearly articulate your new boundary-setting choices, we have provided samples of Agreements, Contracts, Covenants, Scripts, and Letters that can be used in the development of your Plan of Action. This valuable boundary-setting material is available as PDF downloads from our website.

http://www.settingboundariesbooks.com/sanity-support/sanity-materials/

The 8th tab section in your 3-ring Action Plan binder is devoted to notes on your own visions and goals. I encourage you to fill up this section. It's time.

IT'S TIME TO STOP PUTTING YOUR LIFE ON HOLD

Platform is a book written by Michael Hyatt for authors, artists, and creative souls. It's a book written for anyone with a dream. Is that you? Listen to Michael...

Don't listen to that mocking little voice that tells you to be more realistic. Ignore it. You can either accept reality as it is or create it as you wish it to be. This is the essence of dreaming—and thinking big.

Of course, most people don't bother to write down their goals. Instead, they drift through life aimlessly, wondering why their life lacks purpose and significance. I am not saying that committing your goals to writing is the end-game. It's not. But it is the beginning.

Michael Hyatt, *Platform: Get Noticed in a Noisy World* (Nashville, TN: Thomas Nelson, 2012), pages 38 & 39.

...the tragedy in life doesn't lie in not reaching your goal; the tragedy lies in having no goal to reach.

~ Benjamin E. Mays

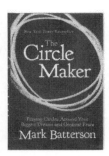

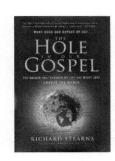

Readers are Leaders

A FEW OF ALLISON'S RECOMMENDED RESOURCES

- *Blue Like Jazz* by Donald Miller
- *Boundaries* by Drs. Henry Cloud & John Townsend
- *Everything* by Mary DeMuth
- *Experiencing God* by Henry T. Blackaby & Claude V. King
- *The Circle Maker* by Mark Batters
- *The Hole in Our Gospel* by Richard Stearns
- *The Purpose Driven Life* by Rick Warren

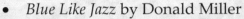

Since ***Setting Boundaries® with Your Adult Children*** was published, God has continued to work in my life, opening my eyes to other areas where I need to set healthy boundaries and find SANITY. Life seems to be a never-ending ebb and flow of alternating periods of triumph and tragedy. The paths on which God places me are often far different than anything I could imagine. I know I'm not alone. That's why, in addition to the Bible, I continue to read life-changing books. It's important to give our brain positive nutrients.

Protecting our hearts, living lives of purpose, and willingly allowing God to use us in a mighty way isn't something we're taught in school. It's not our focus as the challenges in life become daunting. That's why I invite you to visit your church or local bookstore, online retailer, or my website for resources that have helped me make sense of the trials and tests in life and become the person God wants me to be—resources I pray you will find helpful.

Let's join together to make our lives count—to make a difference in the world—starting with making a difference in our own hearts.

Here's an opportunity to apply the "N" Step and **NIP THE EXCUSES IN THE BUD** for why we don't have time (or make time) to read, learn and grow.

GOAL

BEFORE NEXT WEEK'S MEETING

Step Five: What's in Store for Next Week—3 minutes

- **Read:** *Step Three in Gaining SANITY*
  N = NIP Excuses in the Bud (Book Pages 117-125)
- **Complete Week Six** writing assignments in this workbook *before the next session*
- **Jump Start Assignment:** Developing a *written* Plan of Action is a critical step in finding SANITY, yet this is often where the rubber meets the road insofar as commitment and accountability. The bottom line is this, how committed are you to changing your life? We won't "officially" begin discussing Action Plans until Weeks 7 and 10, but completing this **Jump Start Assignment (in addition to your Week 6 homework)** is going to be incredibly helpful. That said, plan to carve out some extra time over the next few days to begin developing your Plan of Action using the detailed guidelines on the following pages. Your plan will be a "Work-in-Progress," but prepare to spend a focused block of time assembling and working on the initial bare-bones of it, and additional time over the next several weeks fine-tuning it. Remember, you're changing habits it has taken years to develop, and your future and the future of your relationship with your adult child is worth the time and effort.

  Pray about this step as you move forward—ask God to guide you.

Plan to bring your 3-ring binder to class next week.

Step Six: CLOSING PRAYER

Thank you, Lord, for bringing me to this place of hope and healing today. Help me overcome the silent shame I've carried about sharing information about my adult child. Help me not to be judgmental when others share their stories. Thank you for giving me this support group to hold me up and intercede on my behalf when my strength is low. Help me be strong as I look at my circumstances objectively and begin to emotionally distance myself from my situation and gain a healthy perspective. Give me wisdom and discernment to make choices based on the facts, not feelings. And Lord, I thank you in advance for guiding my head, heart, and hands as I develop a written plan of action for the areas where I need to set healthy boundaries in a firm and loving way. ~ Amen.

N = NIP EXCUSES IN THE BUD

Allison Bottke's
SANITY Support
SIX STEPS TO HOPE AND HEALING
SettingBoundariesBooks.com

"Nip it! Nip it! Nip it!
Nip excuses in the bud!"
- Barney Fife

WEEK SIX 6

WEEK SIX—*N*—NIP EXCUSES IN THE BUD

Setting Boundaries with Your Adult Children
Step Three in Gaining SANITY:
    NIP Excuses in the Bud (Pages 117-125)

Step One: Open Meeting—5 minutes
1. Cell phones off, take a moment to get quiet and focused
2. Group Reading—The Serenity-SANITY Prayer (Page 16)
3. One Group Member Reads the SANITY Creed (Page 17)

Step Two: Discuss Status of Action Items—30 min. (As identified in Step Four last week.)
How was your week?

Step Three: Group Discussion Points—40 min. (Fill-in-the-blank homework.)

1. As we develop our _____ _____ there must be _____ room for
_____. Our boundaries must be _____. (Page 118)

2. Real healing begins when a parent stops believing the excuses and lies and
insists on the truth. (Page 118) **Follow-up Note from Allison**: However, just because
we *insist* on the truth, doesn't mean we will get it. *So be prepared.*

3. When do you think real healing begins?

_____

_____

_____

4. In what ways have you had blinders on concerning excuses?

_____
_____
_____
_____

5. List your own Top 3 excuses to *Nip in the Bud*:

    1. _____

    2. _____

    3. _____

6. List the Top 3 excuses from your adult child you need to *Nip in the Bud*:

    1. _____

    2. _____

    3. _____

7. Are you ready to handle the conflict and the consequences that may result from *Nipping Excuses in the Bud*?

  ☐ Yes   ☐ No   ☐ Uncertain

8. What did it take for you to draw the line in the sand?

_____
_____
_____
_____

9. Read **Proverbs 4:23**, what is this Scripture saying to you?

_____
_____

**Step Four: Identify Your
   Primary Action Item(s):—10 minutes**

This week I am going to…

If there is time in this session...

If you have time in your group session after **Step Four**, review the additional pages included in this section.

If you are out of time, please move on to **Step Five** and to the *Closing Prayer* in **Step Six**. However, make sure to review the important information (listed below) on your own.

Additional Information:
- Relationships and Responsibilities—page 71
- Setting Boundaries Books—pages 72-73

CLOSING STEPS FIVE & SIX: PAGE 74

Setting Healthy Boundaries
is really all about...

RELATIONSHIPS and RESPONSIBILITIES

One of the most insidious ways Satan has influenced God's children is by keeping them too involved with challenging relationships to care about a relationship with the One who cares the most—Jesus Christ.

After talking with hundreds of women and men about setting healthy boundaries, I'm convinced we have a crippling epidemic that must be addressed. Quite simply, our relationships are out of kilter. We're confused about what is and isn't our responsibility, and we're responding in overly emotional ways that do not honor God or our relationship with His Son. We've lost sight of God's priorities—and when it comes to priorities, God has some very clear standards for how He wants us to live.

- **Allison Bottke**, *Setting Boundaries with Difficult People* (Eugene, OR: Harvest House, 2011), pages 44-45.

It's all about RIGHT RELATIONSHIPS

As a Christian, our number one relationship should be with the *Creator* of our soul—the *Lover* of our heart.

Jesus took the punishment of our sins so we could be restored to a healthy relationship with God. Scripture teaches us about the hierarchy of relationships:

Us & God
Us & Parents
Us & Spouse
Us & Children
Us & Other People
Us & Other Stuff (i.e. work, play, money, time, and even food.)

It's important to be intentional about our priorities.

It's all about TRUSTING GOD

Many of us can truthfully say we love and trust the Lord, read our Bibles, attend church, and tithe regularly. Yet when it comes to our adult children, we do not trust God to handle the circumstances of their lives.

We give God glory, honor, and praise in many areas of our lives—but in this area—when it comes to "helping" our kids—protecting our kids—even sacrificing for our kids—we have demonstrated that we know more than God does, and that's why it's up to us to continually come to their rescue—providing whatever our adult children may need, whenever they need it.

Is this really how God wants us to live?

73

Step Five: What's in Store Next Week—3 minutes

- **Read:** *Step Four in Gaining SANITY:*
  I = IMPLEMENT a Plan of Action (Book Pages 127-136)
- **Complete Week Seven** writing assignments in this workbook *before next session*
- **Special Announcements:** Group Leader/Members

Step Six: CLOSING PRAYER

Heavenly Father, I ask for strength as I resolve to no longer give in to the excuses, lies, and manipulation of my adult child. Open my eyes to see the truth more clearly. Help me respond firmly and lovingly. I confess that sometimes I feel too weak to stop this negative pattern of enabling. I need Your strength and power in my life today to sustain me and keep me standing strong. Help my child understand that my new behavior, new choices, and new responses is coming from a place of love. ~ Amen.

I = IMPLEMENT A PLAN OF ACTION

Allison Bottke's

SANITY Support

SIX STEPS TO HOPE AND HEALING

SettingBoundariesBooks.com

WEEK SEVEN 7

WEEK SEVEN—*I*—IMPLEMENT A PLAN OF ACTION

Setting Boundaries with Your Adult Children
Step Four in Gaining SANITY: IMPLEMENT Rules and Boundaries (Pages 127-135)

Step One: Open Meeting—5 minutes
1. Cell phones off, take a moment to get quiet and focused
2. Group Reading—The Serenity-SANITY Prayer (Page 16)
3. One Group Member Reads the SANITY Creed (Page 17)

Step Two: Discuss Status of Action Items—30 min. (As identified in Step Four last week.)
How was your week?

Step Three: Group Discussion Points—40 min. (Fill-in-the-blank homework.)

1. Establishing a clear set of _____ and _____ is vital when the goal is to heal the hurt our enabling has caused. (Page 127)

2. On pages 130-131, the concept of carrying loads is discussed. We have been carrying too many loads for others. Read these pages and Galatians 6:5 several times to prepare for an Open Discussion in our next session.

3. There are three key areas we need to pray about when it comes to moving forward. List those three areas below: (Pages 131-135)

- D_____
- L_____
- D_____ B_____

4. How will you **DETACH** from the insanity of your own negative behaviors and choices to begin finding SANITY?

_____

_____

_____

5. How can we learn to **LISTEN** with love from a place of strength?

_____

_____

6. Why is **DEFINING BOUNDARIES** a critical component in all healthy relationships?

_____

_____

_____

7. In what areas will you most likely need to identify firm consequences as you define and establish boundaries with your adult child(ren)? (Page 135)

☐ Communication   ☐ Living Arrangements
☐ Finances   ☐ Employment
☐ Family   ☐ Education

8. Grab your Action Plan 3-ring binder and review the next two pages. Prepare to discuss the *"I"* step in SANITY in our next session, *Implementing an Action Plan*. Bring your binder to class.

Step Four: Identify Your Primary Action Item(s):—10 minutes

This week I am going to…
     work on my Action Plan!

SCRIPTURE STRENGTH

I can do everything through Christ who gives me strength.

Philippians 4:13 (NIV)

If there is time in this session...

If you have time in your group session after **Step Four**, review the additional pages included in this section.

If you are out of time, please move on to **Step Five** and to the *Closing Prayer* in **Step Six**. However, make sure to review the important information (listed below) on your own.

Additional Information:
- Jesus, the Original Author of Boundaries—page 79
- Let's Review Our Plan of Action—page 80
- The Components of a Plan of Action—page 81

CLOSING STEPS FIVE & SIX: PAGE 82

Jesus...

the original author of boundaries.

Above all else, guard your heart, for it is the wellspring of life.
Proverbs 4:23

SettingBoundariesBooks.com

Let's review the 3-ring binder we developed back in Week 5.

Grab your 3-ring binder, how far have you traveled on the journey to articulate your thoughts and feelings on paper?

There are no right or wrong answers. This is where you give voice to how you want to live and what you are willing to do to achieve your goals. This is where you listen and Trust the Voice of the Spirit. This is where you begin to identify the possible consequences of setting healthy boundaries (both good and bad). This is where you can begin to "see" the real journey to SANITY beginning.

These notes are for your eyes only (and your spouse if applicable). Eventually, you will type the key points from various sections into the final Plan of Action that depending on your situation you may or may not present to your adult child for their signature (although everyone needs to develop a Plan of Action, not every plan needs to be presented to an adult child.)

Establish a Timeline and place it in the "TO DO" section, include dates for:

PLAN OF ACTION TIMELINE

DATE   **ITEM**

Week 5   Get 3-ring binder and supplies
_____   Begin to write stream-of-consciousness notes
_____   Type first draft of Plan of Action (or find someone to help)
_____   Fine-tune Plan of Action draft and share it with SANITY Support group
_____   Talk w/ counselor/therapist re: Plan of Action (if applicable)
_____   Identify other key timeline areas as applicable
_____   Decide on date to complete Plan of Action
_____   Decide on date to present Plan of Action to adult child (if applicable)

Remember to always begin and end your Plan of Action work with prayer, asking God to direct your path and to give you the peace of conviction that the steps you are taking and the choices you are making are pleasing to Him. Pray, "God, Thy will be done."

A **Plan of Action** will work in any situation or circumstance where healthy boundaries need to be established. Including but not limited to the following. Check those that apply to you.

☐ Adult child is living in your home (under your roof)
☐ Adult child is living in a home you own (located elsewhere)
☐ Adult child lives in their own home/apt. (that you may/may not subsidize)
☐ Adult child lives on campus at college (that you may/may not subsidize)
☐ Adult child has children of their own (who may/may not be your grandkids)

In Week 10 we will really get down to brass tacks in our Plan of Action. However, feel free to continue writing in your 3-ring binder if you have already started to work on this critical area. It's never too soon to begin planning. (Pages 164-165)

The Components of a Plan of Action

1. Statement of Purpose
2. Changes being implemented
3. What you will do
4. What you will not do
5. Resources available
6. Transition care package

In developing our Plan of Action, we'll look at defining and establishing boundaries with our adult children, as well as identifying firm consequences, in the following areas: (Page 135)

- Communication
- Living Arrangements
- Finances
- Employment
- Family
- Education

A Note from Allison about the "I" Step in SANITY...

God has already mastered the *"I"* step in **SANITY**.
He has already *Implemented a Plan of Action*
for His children, and it's called; **The Bible**.
Filled with wisdom, guidance, and yes,
rules and regulations, it also clearly defines
the consequences of poor choices.
Yet more important, **God's Word** gives us the hope,
healing, peace, and joy we long for—and
the unconditional love we need.

About Scripts (Page 163)

As the SANITY Support outreach has grown, so has reader feedback. Many parents are choosing to write these "scripts" as letters to their adult children. Pray about your choice. Write your scripts (or letters) as though you are talking to your adult child in the specific situation identified. Once you've finished your scripts, practice reading them aloud. Share your scripts with fellow SANITY Support members for feedback. Prepare what you'll say to your kids if they...

a. Ask for money
b. Become abusive
c. Bring drugs into your home
d. Come home under the influence of alcohol or other substances
e. Refuse to follow established boundary guidelines
f. Other situations applicable to your circumstances

BEFORE NEXT WEEK'S MEETING

Step Five: What's in Store for Next Week—3 minutes

- **Read:** *Step Five in Gaining SANITY:*
  *T = **TRUST** Your Instincts* (Book Pages 137-141)
- **Complete Week Eight** writing assignments in this workbook *before next session*

Please note that this study guide has been revised since the last printing of the book; *Setting Boundaries with Your Adult Children,* and as such the author (i.e. moi) has elected to subtly revise some of the 6-Steps to SANITY verbiage. I've always declared that the "T" in SANITY is to trust your instincts insofar as the Holy Spirit is leading us. Therefore, I've decided to clearly identify that intention. Now, instead of "Trust Your Instincts," the "T" step in the 6-Steps to SANITY reads:

T = Trust the Voice of the Spirit

Step Six: CLOSING PRAYER

Thank You, Lord, for bringing me to this place where I can see the need to implement new rules and boundaries. The time has come for me to stop talking about how my adult child needs to change. It's time for me to make changes in my own life. Help me to identify the areas where I must change. Give me the strength to detach from my adult child's problems. Help me to release everyone else's problems from my heart and to see with new eyes the areas where I need to change my own heart. Help me learn to listen to Your voice from a place of strength and peace. Help me to define my own boundaries in a firm yet loving manner. ~ Amen.

T = TRUST THE VOICE OF THE SPIRIT

Allison Bottke's

SANITY Support

SIX STEPS TO HOPE AND HEALING

SettingBoundariesBooks.com

WEEK EIGHT 8

Trust

WEEK EIGHT—*T*—TRUST THE VOICE OF THE SPIRIT

Setting Boundaries with Your Adult Children
Step Five in Gaining SANITY:
TRUST Your Instincts (Pages 137-141)

Step One: Open Meeting—5 minutes
1. Cell phones off, take a moment to get quiet and focused
2. Group Reading—The Serenity-SANITY Prayer (Page 16)
3. One Group Member Reads the SANITY Creed (Page 17)

Step Two: Discuss Status of Action Items—30 min. (As identified in Step Four last week.)
How was your week?

Step Three: Group Discussion Points—40 min. (Fill-in-the-blank homework.)

1. _____ is a key issue in our faith.

2. We may not trust our adult children—or even ourselves at times—but we need to _____ that God is _____ in _____.

3. What does Scripture teach us in Proverbs 3:5-6 and John 14:16-17?

_____

_____

_____

_____

4. What has the still small voice of the Holy Spirit been telling you concerning the boundary choices you are making (or not making)?

_____
_____
_____
_____

5. Prayer is a key component in communicating with God. We must stop the insanity by intentionally listening to His voice. What are some ways we can do this?

_____
_____
_____
_____

CAUTION: *By ignoring your instincts or intuition, you could open yourself to the possibility of being an accessory to a crime. If you feel your adult child is involved in illegal activity of any kind, trust your God-given instincts and prayerfully listen to the Spirit-filled instructions you receive from God when you pray.*

6. Are you experiencing or fearing a volatile situation that may include your need to address illegal activity—or take legal action? Are you feeling increasing conviction on your heart regarding a reality that is painful to address? If so, prepare to discuss this at the next session. Stop right now and ask God to give you wisdom and discernment.

Step Four: Identify Your Primary Action Item (s):—10 minutes

This week I am going to…

Step Five: What's in Store Next Week—3 minutes

- **Read:** *Step Six in Gaining SANITY:*
    Y = YIELD Everything to God (Book Pages 143-152)
- **Complete Week Nine** writing assignments in this workbook *before next session*
- **Special Announcements:** Group Leader/Members

Step Six: CLOSING PRAYER

Father God, I thank You for the gift of Your Holy Spirit—the Spirit of Truth. I thank You that I can lean on You with all of my heart, mind, and soul—even when I don't understand. Thank you for talking to me in the still small voice of my instincts and intuition. Help me learn to trust You and my instincts as I seek the Truth in areas concerning my adult child. Help me find strength to make difficult choices. Give me discerning eyes to see and dependable ears to hear what You are telling me. ~ Amen.

Y = YIELD EVERYTHING TO GOD

Allison Bottke's
SANITY Support
SIX STEPS TO HOPE AND HEALING
SettingBoundariesBooks.com

WEEK NINE 9

WEEK NINE—Y—YIELD EVERYTHING TO GOD

Setting Boundaries with Your Adult Children
Step Six in Gaining SANITY:
> *YIELD Everything to God* (Pages 143-152)

Step One: Open Meeting—5 minutes
1. Cell phones off, take a moment to get quiet and focused
2. Group Reading—The Serenity-SANITY Prayer (Page 16)
3. One Group Member Reads the SANITY Creed (Page 17)

Step Two: Discuss Status of Action Items—30 min. (As identified in Step Four last week.)
How was your week?

Step Three: Group Discussion Points—40 min. (Fill-in-the-blank homework.)

1. ...one thing about being a parent in pain: you realize that the help you need is going to have to come from some _____ _____ than yourself. (Page 143)

2. True healing begins when we make the head-heart connection that we must "_____ ____ and _____ _____" concerning all things, not just the painful situations concerning our adult children. (Page 146)

3. Have you found that you can yield to God, only to find that you have just as quickly "unyielded" without even realizing it? What can you do to be more consistent?

_____
_____
_____

4. Look at Judy Hampton's list on pages 151-152. Is God teaching you any of these same lessons? If so, which ones? Prepare to discuss this in the next class.

_____

_____

_____

_____

5. Read Allison's letter on the next page. Prepare to discuss this in the next class.

_____

_____

Step Four: Identify Your Primary Action Item(s):—10 minutes

This week I am going to…

Only when we let go and let God handle things can true healing and hope come from the ashes of despair.

T. Suzanne Eller, Author,
The Mom I Want to Be:
Rising Above Your Past
to Give Your Kids
a Great Future

Suzie Eller, her granddaughter, and me. 4/2/11

If there is time in this session...

If you have time in your group session after **Step Four**, review the additional pages included in this section.

If you are out of time, please move on to **Step Five** and to the *Closing Prayer* in **Step Six**. However, make sure to review the important information (listed below) on your own.

Additional Information:
- *To You*—A Poem by Christopher Smith —page 91
- The Freedom to Let Go and Let God—pages 92-93

CLOSING STEPS FIVE & SIX: PAGE 94

I received this poem from my son in May 2008 from prison. It was the first poem he ever wrote to me. He was 36 years old. He was 40 when he got out of prison.

TO YOU

By Christopher J. Smith

© 2008

To you Mom, this is true • there is only one • and that one is you.

I'm sorry for the things I did • I should have listened when

you said • reach for your goals and your dreams and the stars •

and not for money, girls, and fast cars.

But I did not listen, so now I must pay • sitting behind these

walls made of granite and clay.

Topped with razor wire • these walls are quite high •

like a bald eagle, I wish I could fly.

Up and over these walls I would soar • then, start a new life • and that is for sure.

But I can't fly • though I wish that I could • so, I'll do my time •

and learn my lesson for good.

So, let's not ponder • let's choose to move on • because life's too short •

and it's not very long.

And when I come out from inside this place •

I know I will live in God's redeeming Grace.

I'll never put you through this hell again • and I'll be the best son •

you'll be proud of me then.

So I wrote this poem especially for you, Mom • and this sure is true •

there is only one • and that one is you.

THE FREEDOM TO LET GO AND LET GOD

BY  Allison Bottke

Allison and Christopher, 1972

Around the Easter season, my thoughts turn to a mother from two thousand years ago—a lady who lived in Nazareth, whose name was Mary. This mother stood at the foot of the cross, watching her firstborn son, Jesus, take his final breath. Oh, how her heart must have broken.

I have often wondered, at what moment did she, as a mom, surrender her will to God? Was it when Jesus was learning to walk and fell, when He sat in the temple with the scholars, or when He fed five thousand from a few fish and loaves of bread?

As she watched Jesus grow up and become independent from her care, did she continually remind herself that God was in control? Did she feel like running after Him as he dragged himself down the dusty Via Dolorosa road toward the cross? How she must have wanted to reach out to Him as the crowds spat on Him, when the guards beat Him and hung Him on a cross. Her arms must have ached with the emptiness. Yet she knew it was time to let Him go.

Many of us make the mistake of holding on too tightly to the reins of our lives—or the lives of our adult children. We must understand that true growth requires letting go.

True growth and healing begins when we make the head-heart connection that we must "let go and let God" concerning *all things*, not just painful situations concerning our adult children. This kind of surrender doesn't mean we are giving up, that we no longer care what happens. On the contrary, it means we relinquish their care to a far greater and infinitely more powerful Caregiver. It means we have come at last to the end of our own self-centeredness and can see the the need to step out of the way of spiritual progress.

When the "letting go" part has been accomplished in our hearts and the "letting God" part becomes the focus of our lives, something amazing begins to happen: we feel free. We may not even realize how imprisoned we have been—not until those fears for our adult children are gone.

Total surrender to God must become a daily practice. We open our hands and hearts—releasing those we love to Him. Yielding to God may be something you do well—time and time again—and then if you are like most of us, you just as quickly "unyield" without even realizing it.

Mary could have tried to protect Jesus. She could have overstepped her boundaries and forced her "motherly opinion" on her son. She could have forbidden Him to go to the Garden of Gethsemane, but she knew He had to fulfill His own destiny and a much higher purpose.

Sometimes we have to let our adult children experience pain and suffering. They must exercise their own choices and experience the full consequences of their actions. Who are we to say if it is the right or wrong direction? Perhaps the journey our adult children are on is exactly the road God wants them to travel to learn essential lessons and become the people He wants them to be. 🤍

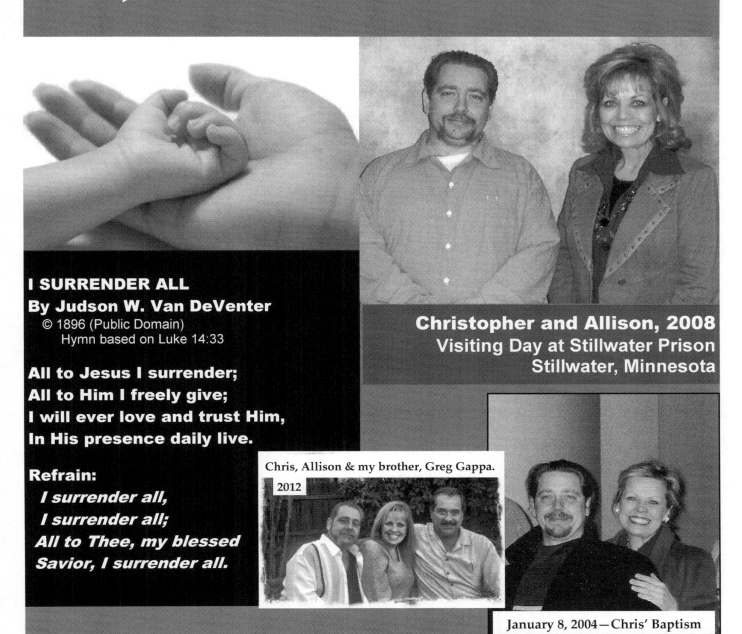

I SURRENDER ALL
By Judson W. Van DeVenter
 © 1896 (Public Domain)
 Hymn based on Luke 14:33

All to Jesus I surrender;
All to Him I freely give;
I will ever love and trust Him,
In His presence daily live.

Refrain:
 I surrender all,
 I surrender all;
All to Thee, my blessed
Savior, I surrender all.

Christopher and Allison, 2008
Visiting Day at Stillwater Prison
Stillwater, Minnesota

Chris, Allison & my brother, Greg Gappa.
2012

January 8, 2004—Chris' Baptism

93

BEFORE NEXT WEEK'S MEETING

Step Five: What's in Store Next Week—3 minutes

- **Read:** *Developing an Action Plan* (Book Pages 153-170)
- **Complete Week Ten** writing assignments in this workbook *before next session*
- Continue working on your Action Plan: *Don't give up!*
- **Special Announcements:** Group Leader/Members

Step Six: CLOSING PRAYER

Heavenly Father, I come before You today with open hands and an open heart. I release my adult child to You. Please help my adult child change the attitudes and behaviors that need to change, and help me see that it is not in my power to change my adult child. The only person I can change is me. I open my heart for You to do the healing necessary in my life. Give me strength as I take the next steps to develop a written Plan of Action. Be with me every step of the way as I transition from the cyclone of chaos to the calm breeze of boundaries. I know You have a purpose for my life. Please help me to see it more clearly. ~ Amen.

DEVELOPING A PLAN OF ACTION

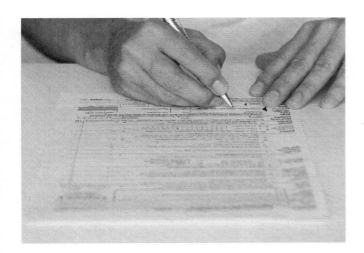

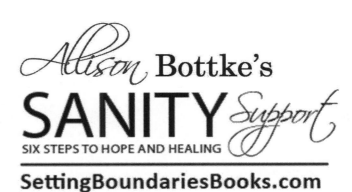

Alison Bottke's
SANITY Support
SIX STEPS TO HOPE AND HEALING

SettingBoundariesBooks.com

WEEK TEN 10

WEEK TEN—DEVELOPING A PLAN OF ACTION

Setting Boundaries with your Adult Children
Developing an Action Plan (Pages 153-170)

Step One: Open Meeting—5 minutes
1. Cell phones off, take a moment to get quiet and focused
2. Group Reading—The Serenity-SANITY Prayer (Page 16)
3. One Group Member Reads the SANITY Creed (Page 17)

Step Two: Discuss Status of Action Items—30 min. (As identified in Step Four last week.)
How was your week?

Step Three: Group Discussion Points—40 min. (Fill-in-the-blank homework.)

1. Allison included enhanced guidelines for Developing an Action Plan at the end of Week 5. We will spend the majority of our time this session discussing our individual plans. But first, let's do a quick review of the Fill-in-the-blank homework for this week.

2. We must come to the table as _____, _____, and _____ adults with a well-developed written plan that clearly indicates our goals. (Page 154)

3. Above all, we must speak this new plan in _____ and not in heated anger or frustration. (Page 154)

4. Remember, we're talking about changing our own _____ not that of our adult child. (Page 155)

5. Why is it important to have a written plan?

_____

_____

6. Have you ever developed a written plan and presented it to your adult child?

☐ Yes ☐ No

7. If you answered "Yes," how will this Action Plan be different?

_____

_____

8. If you are married, does your spouse share your same views on the need to set new boundaries with your adult child (or step-child?)

☐ Yes ☐ No

(If no, please see the personal note from Allison on the next page.)

Step Four: Identify Your Primary Action Item(s):—10 minutes

This week I am going to... fine tune my Plan of Action!

A Reader Speaks Up...

How can I set boundaries with our adult daughter when my husband is the enabler? He doesn't see what he does as a problem. He gives her money, cigarettes, and his car and always has an excuse for her behavior. I am at the end of my rope and considering leaving a 35-year relationship because I can no longer live this way. I need help.

~D

How is Your Plan of Action Progressing?

Week 5
We got a jump start on our Plan of Action.
(Did you develop your 3-ring binder?)

Week 7
We discussed the value of
Implementing a Plan of Action.

Week 10
Here we are at Week Ten,
where are you with your Plan of Action?

If there is time in this session...

If you have time in your group session after **Step Four**, review the additional pages included in this section.

If you are out of time, please move on to **Step Five** and to the *Closing Prayer* in **Step Six**. However, make sure to review the important information (listed below) on your own.

Additional Information:
- Something To Think and Pray About—page 99
- A Personal Note from Allison—page 100
- Is it Time to Reach Out and Get Help? - page 101

CLOSING STEPS FIVE & SIX: PAGE 102

"...for a long time I was unable to see clearly how my own personal issues were contributing to the turmoil in our household. ...It was far less painful to focus on my son and what he needed to do with his life than it was for me to point the spotlight on my own life."
~ Allison Bottke (Page 155)

The Lord gives sight to the blind,
the Lord lifts up those who are bowed down,
the Lord loves the righteous.
Psalm 146:8 (NIV)

&

The Lord also loves those
who say yes with honest authenticity,
and no with firmness and love.

A Personal Note from Allison
There is a difficult topic we need to discuss

If you answered no to question eight on the previous page, this could be a far bigger issue than developing and presenting your adult child with an Action Plan ultimatum. If your spouse is *not* agreeing with you, an already challenging situation can be made even more daunting. It's important for spouses to be supportive of any significant changes being presented to adult children—especially if they are living with you. Developing and presenting an Action Plan to your adult child may be impossible without first taking the spotlight off the adult child and instead focusing on your marriage relationship. This can be scary. *It can also be incredibly healing.*
Sometimes, we've spent so much time and energy focusing on the drama, chaos, and crisis in the lives of our adult children that we've neglected other priority relationships that need help, healing, or perhaps healthy boundaries of their own.

Is it time to shift your relationship priorities?
Ask God to direct your path concerning this possibility.
Ask God to reveal new insight to your mind and heart.

Pray about direction concerning marriage counseling, pastoral counseling, or other professional intervention to begin communicating in a healthy and pro-active way with your spouse.

Remember Matthew 19:26
With God all things are possible.

Christian counseling can help you learn to set firm *and* loving boundaries. There is hope and there is help when a hurting soul and a healing Savior are brought together by a caring Christian counselor. No matter where you live, you can find a licensed professional in your area by contacting the
American Association of Christian Counselors at <u>AACC.net</u>

Is it time to reach out and get help?

Is that still small voice convicting you to take your journey of change a step further and seek the help of a professional counselor?

Don't wait until it's too late

Search online for a licensed professional in your area at the
American Association of Christian Counselors at AACC.net

Life has a way of handing us problems that we are not always prepared to handle. It is important to remember that you don't have to face those problems alone. A trusted counselor can help you find peace and hope when you find yourself overwhelmed or confused by the problems you are facing. Counseling can help you overcome the issues you struggle with, like depression, anger, fear, anxiety, and other dysfunction related to trauma or abuse. It can also help people out of the chaos of co-dependency, enabling, and relationship-communication problems.
~ **Bernis Riley, LPC-S**

Biblically-based Counseling
SoulCareCounselingDFW.com

If you live in the DFW area consider contacting Bernis Riley and SoulCare Counseling

Because I understand my position is that of a layman in the world of Christian counseling, I often invite professional counselors to advise me from time to time, professionals who are better experienced therapeutically to help us on the boundary-setting journey.

Drawing on her experience as a Christian counselor, Bernis Riley provided soul-searching questions and helpful SANITY Support tips at the end of each chapter in *Setting Boundaries with Difficult People, Six Steps to SANITY for Challenging Relationships*. She also wrote sample scripts and letters to help readers approach the difficult person in their life. Bernis conducts a thriving private counseling practice in the DFW area of Texas called, SoulCare Counseling.

SoulCareCounselingDFW.com

Bernis Riley, LPC-S holds a Bachelor of Science degree in Medical Technology from Sam Houston State University and a Master of Arts degree in counseling from Liberty University. Her major experience is in marriage and family therapy and trauma. She is licensed by the state of Texas as a licensed professional counselor supervisor and is also a trained EFT (Emotionally Focused Therapy) therapist. She is a member of the American Association of Christian Counselors and the Christian Counselors of Texas. Bernis is completing a clinical doctorate in Psychology from California Southern University. She and her husband, Dr. Mark Riley, are founders and directors of SoulCare Counseling.

Bernis Riley, LPC-S

Step Five: What's in Store Next Week—3 minutes

- **Read** *Considering the Consequences* (Book Pages 171-183)
- **Complete Week Eleven** writing assignments in workbook *before next session*
- Continue working on your Action Plan
- **Special Announcements:** Group Leader/Members

Step Six: CLOSING PRAYER

Lord, You developed an Action Plan for all Your children, complete with Commandments, Grace, Forgiveness, Mercy, and Love. Your Action Plan also contained Judgment and Discipline. You clearly defined right and wrong. You gave firm, yet loving consequences when we strayed. Help me develop an Action Plan that will be a roadmap, not only to my own freedom but also to the freedom of my adult child. Free me from any negative feelings I may harbor in my heart, and help me outline a Plan of Action that will allow me to live in peace and joy. Allow my adult child to start a journey of self-respect and positive growth. Help me to see clearly if there are other priority relationships I have neglected, and guide me on a path to restore those relationships. ~ Amen

CONSIDERING THE CONSEQUENCES

Allison Bottke's
SANITY Support
SIX STEPS TO HOPE AND HEALING
SettingBoundariesBooks.com

WEEK ELEVEN 11

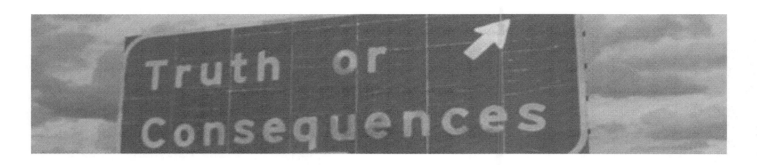

WEEK ELEVEN—CONSIDERING THE CONSEQUENCES

Setting Boundaries with your Adult Children
Considering the Consequences (Pages 171-183)

Step One: Open Meeting—5 minutes
1. Cell phones off, take a moment to get quiet and focused
2. Group Reading—The Serenity-SANITY Prayer (Page 16)
3. One Group Member Reads the SANITY Creed (Page 17)

Step Two: Discuss Status of Action Items—30 min. (As identified in Step Four last week.)
How was your week?

Step Three: Discussion Points—40 min. (Fill-in-the-blank homework.)

1. Healing often comes through _____ _____. (Page 172)

2. We may be _____ our adult children from living out their God given destinies when we _____ them from the consequences of their actions. (Pg. 172)

3. Why is developing a list of possible consequences an important component of your Action Plan?

_____

_____

_____

_____

_____

4. We tend to focus on the potentially negative consequences of implementing our Action Plans. However, there could be positive consequences for our adult children and ourselves. For example:

> Your adult child could enroll in a local community college where God uses one of the instructors to speak life-changing words of encouragement and truth that helps your adult child change the entire course of their life.

> A key area of concern for many parents today is the erosion of their own financial health. Some parents are mortgaging their own homes (and futures) to financially assist their adult children, in some cases, as a result of poor choices they have made (such as overspending or living beyond their means.) When we **STOP the Flow of Money**, a positive consequence could be that we will be able to afford health care in our retirement years.

5. What **decision** is a key ingredient in making the changes needed to stop our enabling behavior? Here's a hint, it's four powerful words on page 183.

D_____ **to** p_____ d_____.

6. Do you think it's ever too late to make that decision?
☐ Yes   ☐ No
(If you answered "*Yes*," turn to page 95 for a revised creed.)

7. Get out your Action Plan 3-ring binder and work on the Consequences section.

Step Four: Identify Your
Primary Action Item(s):—10 minutes

This week I am going to…

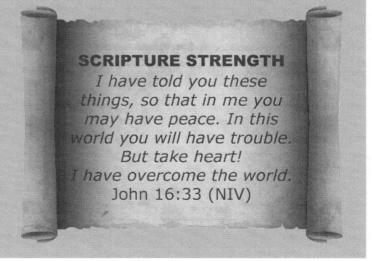

SCRIPTURE STRENGTH
I have told you these things, so that in me you may have peace. In this world you will have trouble. But take heart! I have overcome the world.
John 16:33 (NIV)

If there is time in this session...

If you have time in your group session after **Step Four**, review the additional pages included in this section.

If you are out of time, please move on to **Step Five** and to the *Closing Prayer* in **Step Six**. However, make sure to review the important information (listed below) on your own.

Additional Information:
- A Letter from Allison about Consequences—page 107
- Prepare for the Consequences When the Money Stops—page 108
- Revised INSANITY Support Creed—page 109

CLOSING STEPS FIVE & SIX: PAGE 110

A LETTER FROM ALLISON
ABOUT CONSEQUENCES

When God began to open my eyes to the serious issues I had regarding a lack of healthy boundaries, I was resistant to change, but God helped me realize that I didn't have a choice—*I had to change*. I had to stop accepting responsibility for the choices my son was making, and allow him to fully experience the consequences of his own actions.

This change in my behavior brought its own set of consequences that varied from peace to panic. I wish I could say, when you begin to follow the 6-Steps to SANITY, that your life will be instantly transformed to a pleasurable place of tranquility. However, that's not likely to happen—especially at first.

On the contrary, circumstances may blow up all around you.

That's why it's imperative that you look at all possible consequences and prepare yourself for any scenario. It's time to collectively face the reality of what we've done. *And sometimes what we've done isn't pretty.*

When we no longer accept the consequences for the actions of our adult children, the results can vary greatly. For some, the outcome may barely register as a blip on the radar of life. But for others, it may be a catastrophic crash of the entire screen. When their hands are forced, some adult children may choose to get professional help to turn their lives around. Others may find it more challenging, as they blame us for "picking on them" or for being "too hard on them." And sadly, some may pay the ultimate price of life because of drugs, violence or suicide.

With such varied and frightening possibilities—is it any wonder we are afraid to take the risk? Is it any wonder we have allowed conditions to get so bad? Is it any wonder we have developed an array of elaborate excuses to maintain the status quo?

Yet now that we have embarked on a journey to make different choices and set firm *and* loving boundaries, can we comfortably continue the old way of life that has caused us so much pain for so long? No, we *must* continue to forge ahead and gain SANITY in our lives. We *must* make choices based on rational thinking, not emotional feeling. And we *must* be willing to accept the consequences of our new choices, whatever they may be.

Deciding to parent differently is a key ingredient to change our negatively enabling behaviors. It's never too late to parent differently. It's never too late to turn around. Remember, *God Allows U-Turns*!

And never forget that God is in control. He has a plan, not only for our lives, but for the lives of our adult children. He loves us *all*—and He wants us *all* to be free.

> *With God all things are possible.*
> **Matthew 19:26**

Allison

107

PREPARE FOR THE CONSEQUENCES WHEN WE STOP THE FLOW OF MONEY

When it comes to the dynamics that have contributed to dysfunctional relationships, whether it's with our adult children, aging parents, difficult people, or even with food, every story is unique.

When I first began to set healthy boundaries and find SANITY in my relationship with my adult son, the issues revolved primarily around money. I was going broke subsidizing my son's lifestyle. I was a single mother struggling to make ends meet. I worked extra hours, borrowed money, used credit cards, and did whatever it took to "help" my son. When I *"Stopped the Flow of Money,"* attitudes began to radically shift. No more buying cell phones, used cars, or paying auto insurance. No more paying bail or legal fees. And no more living with Mom when he found himself homeless. I couldn't afford the expense of supporting two adults—especially when one of them wasn't ready, willing, or able to pull his share of the load. But most of all, I couldn't afford what this was doing to my heart, soul, spirit, and mind—and to our relationship. I was beginning to despise my own son. It was an awful way to live.

Sadly, this cycle repeated itself for years—and I'm afraid it still comes up. Old habits are hard to break. It's hard to admit that many of our adult children are only involved in our lives because of their dependence on our income and the safety, comfort, and freedom it provides.

Alas, love is not spelled M-O-N-E-Y, and many of us need to take it out of the equation.

God is in control—not our checking account. We are not God.

When it comes to consequences, we must address four needs to establish healthy boundaries with our adult children.

1. The need to overcome the often paralyzing fear of consequences.
2. The need to accept that there *will be* consequences and we must be willing to live with them.
3. The need to prepare for possible consequences—both positive and negative.
4. The need to focus on the consequences pertaining to our lives, not just on the lives of our adult children. We matter to God just as much as they do.

We've been so busy taking care of our adult children, many of us have no idea about God's purpose for our own lives.

REVISED **INSANITY** SUPPORT CREED

To be read daily in the event you decide to maintain the status quo or to move backward instead of forward. *(Substitute him/her as needed.)*

I cannot change anything about my life or about the choices I make. I am unable to parent differently. Beginning today, I am resigning myself to the fact that neither my adult child, nor I will ever be able to rise above our current circumstances. It's not my responsibility to do anything to proactively change our challenging relationship. I will be forever destined to live a life of insanity as I continue to accept responsibility for the choices my adult child makes and to refuse to change my own. I do not love myself or my adult child enough to let go. I cannot allow my adult child or myself to experience growing pains. I'm not ready, willing, or able to let God do a good work in me or in my adult child. There's no way I can learn how to be firm and loving at the same time. This old dog is incapable of learning any new tricks.

Therefore, I will stay on the gerbil wheel of INSANITY and willingly allow the enemy to continue controlling my life.

The choices we make can change the story of our life. Will we choose *insanity* or *SANITY*?

BEFORE NEXT WEEK'S MEETING

Step Five: What's in Store for Next Week—3 minutes

- **Read** *Other Vital Issues and Epilogue* (Book Pages 185-207)
- Complete **FINAL Week Twelve** reading assignments in this workbook before next session. **<u>NOTE:</u> THERE ARE NO WRITING ASSIGNMENTS.**
- **Special Announcements:** Group Leader/Members

Step Six: CLOSING PRAYER

Father God, I welcome Your presence right now in my heart and my mind. As I step closer to being the kind of loving parent you want me to be, the truth of the possible consequences frightens me. I know You have a purpose for the life of my adult child. I'm asking You, Lord, to keep him safe as he begins this new journey in his life. Send people into his life to help him learn responsibility for his actions. Help me stay strong when the consequences are painful. Help me keep my eyes focused on You whenever the waters of change threaten to capsize my life. Change is sometimes painful. Yet without it we cease to grow—we cease to live a full life. I want to live a full life. I want my adult child to live a full life. Yet I need to remember that my adult child may never change. But I have. Thank you, Lord, for helping me set healthy boundaries. Thank you for bringing me to a place where I'm focusing on understanding Your purpose for my life. Thank You, Lord, for helping me jump off the gerbil wheel of insanity and find SANITY in Your loving arms. ~ Amen

OTHER VITAL ISSUES AND CLOSING

Allison Bottke's

SANITY Support

SIX STEPS TO HOPE AND HEALING

SettingBoundariesBooks.com

Final Session

WEEK TWELVE 12

WEEK TWELVE—OTHER VITAL ISSUES AND IN CLOSING

Setting Boundaries with Your Adult Children
Read Other Vital Issues and Epilogue (Pages 185-207)

Step One: Open Meeting—5 minutes
1. Cell phones off, take a moment to get quiet and focused
2. Group Reading—The Serenity-SANITY Prayer (Page 16)
3. One Group Member Reads the SANITY Creed (Page 17)

Step Two: Discuss Status of Action Items—30 min. (As identified in Step Four last week.)
This is our last session, how have you been—and how are you doing?

Step Three: Group Discussion Points—40 min.
1. Discuss the value of "Staying Connected" on page 113
2. Discuss (perhaps read aloud) Allison's letter on pages 114-115
3. Briefly review the reader comments on page 116
4. Distribute Program Evaluation forms as mentioned on page 117 (Take 5 minutes to complete the forms and return them to the Group Leader.)
5. Complete **Step Four** on page 119 (returning to pages 28-29)
6. Complete your Certificate on page 120
7. Briefly discuss the available material in the Resources section (pages 123-130)
8. Please share pages 128-129 with your Pastors and Church Leaders.
9. Any personal feedback from Group Leader and/or Group Members?
10. Close this final session with **Steps Five & Six** on page 122

Have you been blessed by participating in this SANITY Support Group? If so, please visit our Facebook community and share your experiences. Encourage others to start or attend a SANITY Support Group in their community. Please pray about leading your own 12-week session.

The "A" Step in SANITY is important even after you complete this 12-week journey. *Stay Connected* with your SANITY Support Group and with readers from around the world on our Facebook fan page. "Like" us soon, if you haven't done so yet.

Stay Connected!

VIA OUR FACEBOOK COMMUNITY

Facebook.com/AuthorAllisonBottke

THE 12-WEEK SESSION MAY BE OVER BUT YOUR LIFE HAS JUST BEGUN!

I pray that any negative feelings of anger, fear or confusion you had on Week One have been replaced by hopeful feelings of possibility and joy on this Week Twelve. I also pray that God has provided abundantly for your needs, and that you have received far more than you imagined possible when you began this journey to find SANITY.

As we come to the end of our twelve-week program, I can't stress enough the need to fully depend on God to give us wisdom, guidance, and strength to continue this journey. We've come a long way in twelve weeks. We've learned about changing our choices—and how we must change our responses to the choices our adult children make.

We've learned that we can't change our kids—and the fact is, they may never change. It's a sad thing to acknowledge—but it may be true. However, the opposite could also be true. When we decide to trust God and His Word, and when we develop a backbone that is firm, straight, *and* loving, the people we love may change. It can happen.

And we do love them. No matter how angry they make us. No matter how they may break our hearts. That's why we've made so many poor choices. But no more.

Our negative enabling days are behind us. We've learned we are not bad parents if we say no.

It's not easy to be firm *and* loving—but when we depend on God's grace, wisdom, and mercy to guide us, amazing things happen!

Believe me, I know what it feels like to want to turn away from my son and never deal with his issues again. I spent many years mired in the muck of his drama, chaos, and crisis. But he's my son, and I love him. I can't turn away from him. However, God opened my eyes to see that loving my son doesn't mean I have to accept his choices, nor does it mean I have to bear the acute financial or emotional responsibility for them.

Deciding to parent differently is a daily choice, as is my desire to make my relationship with the Lord a first priority in my life.

Let's use this final session to talk about how far we've come in twelve weeks, and how we will stay strong as we continue the journey to set healthy boundaries in our relationships.

> *Don't be afraid, for I am with you. Don't be discouraged, for I am your God. I will strengthen you and help you. I will hold you up with my victorious right hand.*
>
> Isaiah 41:10 (NLT)

Before we close in prayer for our last time together, I encourage you to pray about continuing your group, either by repeating the entire twelve-week session, or perhaps meeting less frequently, such as once a month for a potluck dinner. No doubt, what you've shared and learned in this group has changed your lives, and the bond you have developed does not have to stop here.

If you are the Group Leader, thank you for allowing God to use you in a mighty way. I hope this has been a life-changing experience. The part our Group Leaders play is a critical component for the success that men and women are experiencing in SANITY Support Groups around the country. God bless you for giving so unselfishly these past weeks.

Please pray about leading another twelve-week session, inviting new members, perhaps. As parents struggle with this painful topic, the need for SANITY is great.

Perhaps you are a Group Member feeling convicted that God is calling you to start your own SANITY Support Group. If so, all the material you need is in the Leader Guide included at the end of this Study Guide.

In closing, my prayer is that you will all continue to embrace the newfound SANITY you've discovered. That you will begin to use these 6-Steps as a way to address any challenging situation, and that you will share these steps with others.

Also, please share the important information on pages 112-113 with your Pastor and church leaders.

In the book *Shade of His Hand*, author Oswald Chambers wrote, "It is in the middle that human choices are made; the beginning and the end remain with God. The decrees of God are birth and death, and in between those limits man makes his own distress or joy."

My deepest desire is that you experience great joy by choosing to follow the Creator of the universe and the Lover of your heart and soul. And never forget that the choices we make really can change the story of our life.

May God's peace be with you always.

Allison Bottke

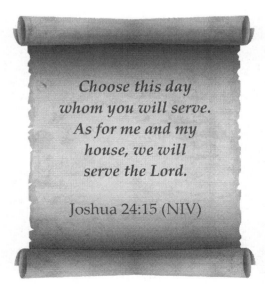

Choose this day whom you will serve. As for me and my house, we will serve the Lord.

Joshua 24:15 (NIV)

**2013 Christmas Eve service at church
Allison and Christopher**

...There are many excellent points in your book. For us, two key points led the list. First, we needed to accept responsibility for our own actions by acknowledging the poor parenting decisions we had made, and apologize to our son for that, which we have done. We started with your sample script (p.94) and made it our own in a letter to our son. Second, we needed to accept our son for who he is, while stopping our enabling behavior. Again, that was not easy. But, as you point out, our prayer is that in the course of our new journey, our son will find his way as well; and, that we all will live our lives in peace and happiness. With the help of your book, our counselor, each other, and God – yes there was and continues to be a great deal of prayer – my wife and I have stopped our enabling behavior while, thankfully, maintaining a strong, loving relationship with our son. God bless you, *L.D.*

Today I saw you on the TBN channel, and I had this overwhelming need to share with you and to thank God for people like you that help us know we are not alone. Thank you for your courage to reach out to those of us in pain. Respectfully, *S.A.*

...I couldn't wait to finish reading your book before I thanked you for it. I have felt so alone for so long – so guilty, never being able to do enough because of the mistakes I made with my children, but constantly trying, and just making things worse. Your book is the first book I have come across that nailed what I am going through. I thank God for you and for this book. Thanks again! *M.W.*

...I sat in the bookstore reading your book and crying, feeling like it was my story and also my heart breaking for you as a mother. I finished the book the next day and let me tell you, I felt so empowered and still do. I will read it over and over again daily to make sure I keep everything fresh in my mind and keep reminding myself not to let fear keep me from doing the right thing and from letting my son take responsibility for his own actions and accepting the consequences of his choices without my intervening. Thank you! *M.S.*

...Thank you so much for writing the book, *Setting Boundaries with Your Adult Children*. I bought it from a bookstore here in Mississauga, Ontario, Canada and I read it out loud word for word with my husband on a Saturday and it took us 8 hours with some breaks! We are Christian parents and could not put the book down because it related so much to what we are going thru. Thanks & God bless you, *M.*

Thank you for helping me know I'm not alone, and for helping me to realize that I'm not an evil, horrid person for being so tough. Thank you for helping me understand that there is still hope for my son, and that it is okay for me to want a better life. *T.R.*

Please provide...

Feedback

GROUP LEADER WILL DISTRIBUTE A PROGRAM EVALUATION FORM

Allison reads every one of these forms, so please take a few minutes to share your feedback with her.

We will take 5-minutes to complete these forms.
Return completed forms to the Group Leader
who will mail them to Allison.

TODAY WILL NEVER COME AGAIN.
Be a blessing.
Be a friend.
Encourage someone.
Take Time To Care.
Let your words heal, and not wound.

It *is* possible to be firm *and* loving at the same time. Setting healthy boundaries does not mean you do not care.

STEP FOUR: Identify How You Feel Now

Let's turn back to pages 28-29 in week one and look at what we wrote. Then, let's take a few minutes to write down how we feel today.

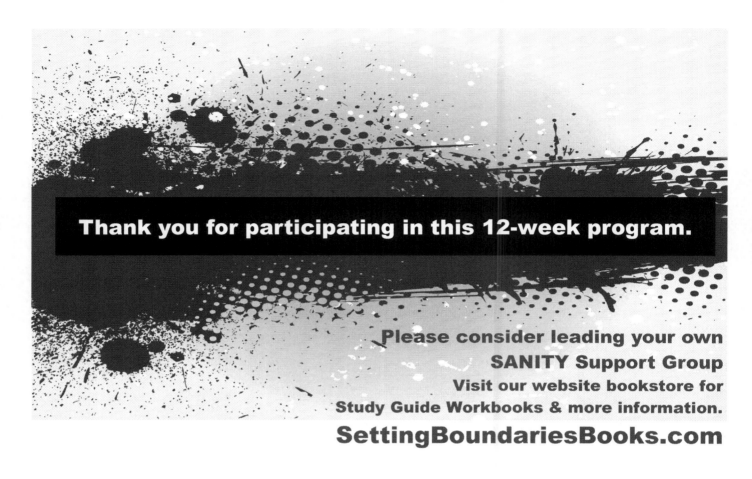

Thank you for participating in this 12-week program.

Please consider leading your own
SANITY Support Group
Visit our website bookstore for
Study Guide Workbooks & more information.
SettingBoundariesBooks.com

CONGRATULATIONS!

You have successfully completed
6-Steps to SANITY and 12-Weeks to Freedom

_____

Your Name

_____

Date

Allison **Bottke**

SANITY *Support*
SIX STEPS TO HOPE AND HEALING
SettingBoundariesBooks.com

God

...the original designer
of boundaries

Visit us at:
SettingBoundariesBooks.com
Facebook.com/AuthorAllisonBottke
Facebook.com/SanitySupportForYoungWomen

Step Five: What's in Store for the Future...
Continued growth and SANITY in ALL of our relationships!

Step Six: CLOSING PRAYER

Heavenly Father, there are so many variables in life. Help me understand that the only constant in my life is Your love for me. Help me see the trials and tribulations of life as growing pains that will bring me closer to You. Lord, please fill my heart, mind, and soul with the knowledge that it's never too late for You to restore the life of my adult child. You have restored my life and helped me on a journey of change that has brought me hope and healing. You can do the same for my adult child. Thank you for leading me to this group and for the friendships you have forged along the way. I know my life is built on a solid rock that can never be moved, and I pray for opportunities to share the truth of your love—and of SANITY—with others. I love You, Lord, and I yield my life and the life of my adult child to You. ~ Amen

HELPFUL RESOURCES

Check out the following pages to help strengthen your SANITY muscles! Feel free to photocopy and distribute the pages in this section.

Resources

STATEMENT OF FAITH

What We Believe...

About God: God is the creator and the ruler of the universe. There is only one, true holy God. He eternally exists in three personalities: The Father, The Son, and The Holy Spirit. These three are co-equal and are one God. Genesis 1: 1,26-27, 3:22; Psalm 90:2; Matthew 28:19; I Peter 1:2; II Corinthians 13:14.

About Jesus: Jesus Christ is the Son of God. He is co-equal with the Father (God). Jesus lived on earth by a miraculous conception and virgin birth. He lived a sinless human life and offered Himself as the perfect sacrifice for the sins of all people by dying on a cross. He arose from the dead after three days to demonstrate His power over sin and death. He ascended to Heaven's glory and will return again to earth to reign as King of Kings and Lord of Lords. Matthew 1:22-23; Isaiah 9:6; John 1:1-5, 14: 10-30; Hebrew 4:14-15; I Corinthians 15:3-4; Romans 1:3-4; Acts 1:9-11; I Timothy 6:14-15; Titus 2:13; John 14:6; Hebrews 13:8.

About the Holy Spirit: The Holy Spirit is co-equal with the Father (God) and the Son of God (Jesus). He is present in the world to make people aware of their need for Jesus Christ. He also lives in every Christian from the moment of salvation. He provides the Christian with power for living, understanding of spiritual truth, and guidance in doing what is right. The Christian seeks to live under His control daily. II Corinthians 3:17; John 16:1-13, 14:16-17; Acts 1:8; I Corinthians 2:12, 3:16; Ephesians 1:13; Galatians 5:25; Ephesians 5:18.

About the Bible: The sole basis for our belief is the Bible. The Bible is God's Word to all people. It was written by human authors under the supernatural guidance of the Holy Spirit. It is the supreme source of truth for Christian beliefs and living. Because it is inspired by God, the Scriptures are infallible and inerrant in the original manuscripts. They are the final authority on all matters of faith and practice. II Timothy 3:16-17; II Peter 1:21; James 1:22; Hebrews 4:12; Romans 1:16-17.

About Salvation: Because of the sin of Adam, all have sinned and are separated from God. The result is eternal death and separation from God. Through the death and resurrection of Jesus Christ, however, we have the gift from God to all people, Salvation. We can never make up for our sin by self-improvement or good works. Only by trusting in Jesus Christ as God's offer of forgiveness can people be saved from sin's penalty. Eternal life begins the moment one receives Jesus Christ into his life by faith. Romans 6:23; Ephesians 2:8-9; John 14:6, 1:2, Titus 3:5; Galatians 3:26; Romans 5:1,8; John 1:12; Romans 10:13; Revelation 3:20.

CALL TO SALVATION

My U-Turn toward God began in 1989 when, at the age of 35, I had reached the end of my rope. For years, I had filled my days with busy, take-charge tasks. I filled my nights with alcohol, pot, parties, and self-destruction. I filled my soul with empty pursuits. One summer evening I was taking a walk in my neighborhood when I noticed people going into the neighborhood church. Suddenly my legs developed a mind of their own, virtually propelling me up the steps and through the doors. Alone in the church balcony, I looked toward the pulpit and saw a statue of Jesus with outstretched arms, and He was looking right at me. Hot tears fell down my cheeks as emotions I could not explain filled my heart and soul. When the Pastor began to speak, it was a message of being lost, without direction, without hope, without faith—and how it did not have to be like that. He talked of how we needed only to listen to the Holy Spirit and ask the Lord Jesus Christ to come into our hearts, and He would be there—just like that. My walk with the Lord started that day, a day that forever changed my life. ~ **Allison Bottke**

The Bible Says: "Behold, what manner of love the Father hath bestowed upon us, that we should be called the sons of God." – 1 John 3:1

Through Jesus Christ, the line of communication between God and you has been opened, and you can talk directly with Him in prayer. Is it time you spoke to God? This conversation is between you and God alone. After you have sincerely prayed the prayer below, write today's date below as a reminder of the moment when you accepted Jesus Christ as your personal Savior and thereby received Eternal Life!

Dear Heavenly Father, I know that I am a sinner, and I ask you to forgive me. I believe Christ died for me, and I want to turn from my sins. Jesus, come into my heart and be my personal savior. I promise to obey and follow you all the days of my life. In Jesus' name, amen.

Then, if you feel like sharing this wonderful moment with your new family, please let us know so we can rejoice with you! You can email me at Allison@AllisonBottke.com

How to be Born Again...

1. **BELIEVE** that Jesus Christ is the Son of the Almighty God.
2. **BELIEVE** that because Jesus Christ gave His life on the cross to free you from sin's penalty, you can be forgiven.
3. **INVITE** the Lord Jesus to come into your life.
4. **ACCEPT** God's forgiveness and His peace.

> *My New Life Began:*
>
> _____(date)

Share your decision with us!
Facebook.com/AuthorAllisonBottke

GOD HAS A POSITIVE ANSWER

YOU SAY	GOD SAYS	BIBLE VERSES
It's impossible	All things are possible	Luke 18:27
I'm too tired	I will give you rest	Matthew 11:28-30
Nobody really loves me	I love you	John 3:1 & John 3:34
I can't go on	My grace is sufficient	2 Corinthians 12:9 & Psalm 91:15
I can't figure things out	I will direct your steps	Proverbs 3:5-8
I can't do it	You can do all things	Philippians 4:13
I'm not able	I am able	2 Corinthians 9:8
It's not worth it	It will be worth it	Romans 8:28
I can't forgive myself	I forgive you	1 John 1:9 & Romans 8:1
I can't manage	I will supply all your needs	Philippians 4:19
I'm afraid	I have not given you a spirit of fear	2 Timothy 1:7
I'm always worried and frustrated	Cast all your cares on ME	1 Peter 5:7
I'm not smart enough	I give you wisdom	1 Corinthians 1:30
I feel all alone	I will never leave you or forsake you	Hebrews 13:5

The Attributes of God

GOD is Eternal

GOD is Faithful

GOD is Gracious

GOD is Good

GOD is Holy

GOD is Infinite

GOD is Immutable

GOD is Just

GOD is Love

GOD is Merciful

GOD is Omnipotent

GOD is Omnipresent

GOD is Self-Sufficient

GOD is Sovereign

GOD is Transcendent

GOD is Wise

ATTENTION
Pastors and Church Leaders

Help those you care about learn how to set firm *and* loving boundaries

As you most likely know, parents and grandparents around the country are struggling emotionally, spiritually and financially—living in chaos from one crisis to another, a result of choices being made (or not made) by their adult children. Or rather, how they themselves are responding to their choices.

Countless parents and grandparents live from drama to drama, basing their own choices on wanting desperately to help their adult children, and yet their repeated attempts to help have not brought the desired results. The vicious cycle of parental enabling has reached epidemic proportion with catastrophic consequences. *This is not how God wants us to live.*

You know the stories. You've heard about the ongoing drama more than once. You know something must change—and it's not just the adult child. How do you help struggling parents understand? **Help those you shepherd to find SANITY in insane situations.** Help those you care about to understand the difference between positive helping and negative enabling. You can help parents and grandparents find hope, healing, and freedom from the bondage of poor boundaries that have held them prisoner for so long.

Please pray about sharing the boundary message from the books in the *Setting Boundaries* ® series from Harvest House Publishers. And please, let me know how I can help you do that.

God's peace,

Allison Bottke

Visit: SettingBoundariesBooks.com

**A person without self-control
is like a city with broken-down walls.**

Proverbs 25:28 (NLT)

How Pastors and Leaders in the Church Community Can Help . . .

1. Share *Setting Boundaries® with Your Adult Children* with your church leaders and members. This is a powerful resource with concrete steps to break enabling patterns.

2. Consider preaching a sermon series on boundaries. Use boundary stories from the Bible and from the book as examples.

3. Encourage your church to start a **SANITY Support Group.** This is an excellent way to strengthen your church family and to increase your community outreach.

> **NOTE:** Because of the epidemic of enabling, people are desperate to find hope, healing and answers. Hosting a **SANITY Support Group** can be a powerful way to reach your community demographic and introduce them to your church family.

4. Mention the *Setting Boundaries®* book series in your church newsletter, bulletin, on your web site, and/or in blogs or e-zines.

5. Ask your church bookstore to sell books in the *Setting Boundaries®* series.

6. Pray for **Allison Bottke** as she continues to share **SANITY** with readers around the world. Consider inviting her to your church to speak.

> **NOTE:** Allison invites Pastors and Church Leaders to contact her directly about this at: Allison@AllisonBottke.com. Type these words in the subject line: **PASTOR REQUEST**.

7. Ask the Lord to show you ways that He wants you to share this important topic with your church and community. *Tell someone in need, help change a life.*

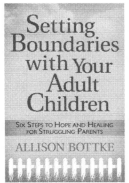  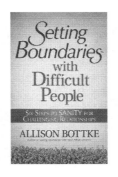  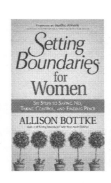 

Additional topics currently in development.
SettingBoundariesBooks.com

Faith is not believing that God can, it is knowing that God will.

SettingBoundariesBooks.com ©

LEADER GUIDE

Thank you and God bless you for being a SANITY Support Group Leader!

*I will instruct you and
teach you in the way you
should go; I will counsel
you and watch over you.*

Psalm 32:8

*And we know that in all things
God works for the good of those who love Him,
who have been called according to His purpose.*

Romans 8:28

Dear Group Leader:

When I wrote *Setting Boundaries® with Your Adult Children*, I felt God was using me to address an epidemic issue that countless parents in pain (just like me) were facing. Now, He is using you to continue this outreach. Thank you for accepting the call to lead a 12-week SANITY Support session in your community.

If you feel led by God to accept this responsibility, you can trust Him to equip and enable you to accomplish the task, no matter where you are on your own journey to set healthy boundaries and find SANITY. You can trust that God is in control, and He has a divine plan and purpose for bringing you to this special place of guiding His children on this courageous journey to learn how to be firm and loving at the same time.

Your role as a Group Leader is to facilitate the group learning process through weekly reading, studying and sharing. As we know, it is the Holy Spirit that is the Teacher, thank you for being the instrument through which the Spirit can work. God has placed you here for such a time as this.

And thank you for your support, encouragement, commitment, and prayers. You are making a difference!

God bless and keep you.

Allison

"...And who knows but that you have come to your royal position for such a time as this?"

Esther 4:14 (NIV)

LEADER GUIDE
TABLE OF CONTENTS

~ The End ~

Leading a SANITY Support Group

SANITY Support Group Leaders are parents, grandparents, men, women, married, or single. They are stay-at-home moms, business professionals, or blue collar workers. Some are pastors and others are licensed counselors or therapists. In all cases, Group Leaders are compassionate volunteers who feel in their heart and soul that this is something they have been called to do—for such a time as this.

If you feel led to assemble and/or lead a SANITY Support Group in your community, please know we will do everything in our power to equip and empower you.

As we implement the first step to STOP our enabling behavior (the "S" Step in SANITY,) it's vital that we apply the "A" Step, and ASSEMBLE Supportive People. Experiencing the support of others is crucial. Parents in pain need understanding, encouragement, and *loving accountability* from others who have traveled this painful journey and come out on the other side—or, from those who are currently walking the journey with us.

There is no required minimum or maximum number of group member participants, however we recommend that large groups break up into smaller cell groups with a maximum of 10-12 people. Your small groups can meet in your home, church, business, storefront, school, or local community center. You can have meetings during the day or in the evening. Your group can meet on weekdays or on the weekend. You may have an "Open" (public) meeting, allowing new members to join at the beginning of the 12-week session, or a "Closed"(private) meeting where your members are personally invited by you—the choice is yours.

Group Leaders are asked to commit to facilitating one 90-minute session every week for 12 consecutive weeks. At the end of the 12 weeks, you may choose to conduct another session, pass-on the leadership of the group to another volunteer, or disband your group entirely—again the choice is yours.

Additional Group Leader Requirements:

* Agree to follow the Meeting Guidelines as outlined in this Member/Leader Guide.

* Purchase your own copy of the book; *Setting Boundaries with Your Adult Children*, and an original copy of this combination SANITY Support Member/Leader Guide.

* Ensure that every Group Member has their own *original copy* of the book as well as an *original copy* of this Study Guide.

##

Please be aware that many Group Members will be in the habit of talking about the drama, chaos, and crisis in the lives of their adult children, and the entire 90-minute session could be devoted to discussing only this. But this is a habit we are trying to break; remember, it isn't about the issues our adult children have, it's *how we respond* to their issues. Step Two of every weekly assignment is; "How was *your* week," not "How was your adult child's week." This isn't being selfish. This is being healthy.

There may also be times when a Group Member (or perhaps even yourself) will be tempted to say something like this to another member, *"You really need to pack his bags and throw him out!"* or perhaps, *"You need to stop giving her money."* However, while these things may indeed be true, it is not our place to tell anyone what they "need to do." It's up to God to convict us of His will—and of the changes He wants us to make in our lives.

There is a fine line between accountability and judgment. Group Members are encouraged to share personal insight, but in a way that does not put pressure on another member.

An effective Group Leader will strive to be aware of times when a Group Member may be violating the Meeting Guidelines (usually unknowingly) and gently redirect the group by referencing guideline sections such as: Sharing, Sensitivity, Advice and Judgment, Venting and such. In fact, during the reading of the Meeting Guidelines in Week One, you may wish to give an example of *what not to do* after Advice and Judgment, and perhaps ask for Group Member feedback on this topic.

A significant part of the success of Alcoholics Anonymous (A.A.) is their requirement that "Crosstalk" be avoided in all group meetings. This has been addressed in Item 7 of our Meeting Guidelines, but you may have to stay on top of this during every session. People mean well, but this can become a touchy issue...

From time to time, Group Leaders are encouraged to ask for volunteer readers. However, there are locations in this study when it's best for the Group Leader to read aloud, particularly during the Week One Orientation. (Remember, you've had time to prepare, many Group Members have not.)

As the Group Leader, it is your responsibility to keep the group moving, using the timeframes indicated on the Weekly Agenda. This may sometimes be challenging, especially if a Group Member is going through a particularly rough patch. In these cases, pray for guidance and let the Spirit lead you regarding how/when to proceed.

And last but not least, if there is time at the end of your weekly session, please review the additional pages included at the end of some weeks before the Closing Prayer. If there isn't time, encourage Group Members to read any additional pages on their own the following week.

And this is my prayer: that your love may abound more and more in knowledge and depth of insight.
Philippians 1:9

SANITY MAKES A COMEBACK!

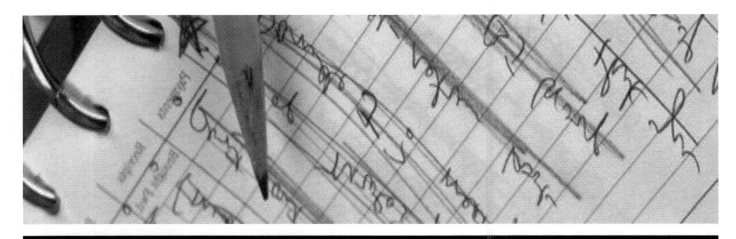

SANITY Support Group Leader Checklist

YOUR FIRST STEPS

☐ Read (or re-read) the book; *Setting Boundaries® with Your Adult Children.*

☐ Find a location to meet. Make sure there is ample room to park outside as well as to sit comfortably inside.

☐ Decide whether your 12-week session will be "Open" (public) or "Closed" (private) and when it will be held. If your session is Closed, personally invite your Group Members and skip the next two steps.

FOUR TO SIX WEEKS BEFORE YOUR 12-WEEK SESSION BEGINS

☐ Photocopy the **Press Release** (page 171) and send completed copies to your local newspaper and radio stations to announce your group. Or scan it and send via email or blog. You are looking for free advertising in Community Calendar listings.

☐ Photocopy the **Invitation Flyer** (page 170) and post it on public bulletin boards at local grocery stores, banks, community recreation centers, senior centers, churches, schools, and businesses.

☐ Encourage confirmed/potential Group Members to purchase a copy of the book on their own. Books are widely available at bookstores and online. Or, you may wish to coordinate this with your church bookstore or a local bookstore to make sure they have copies on hand.

☐ Encourage confirmed/potential Group Members to go online and purchase their Study Guide materials individually from our online bookstore (via Amazon.com.) Or, you may wish to collect money from Group Members and place one group order to take advantage of any quantity and/or shipping rate discounts. **Make sure to place your online order in plenty of time for the start of your group.**

☐ Familiarize yourself with the material contained in this Member/Leader Guide, especially in Week One.

☐ Begin your own SANITY Journal. Record how God may already be working in your personal growth as well as in the development of your group. (Your personal journey is just as important to God.)

ONE WEEK BEFORE YOUR 12-WEEK SESSION BEGINS

☐ Distribute materials to Group Members either beforehand or at the first meeting.

☐ Assemble meeting supplies.

Supplies to Provide at Every Meeting:
- Name Tags (until familiar)
- Pens/Pencils
- Box(es) of Tissue
- Clock (if none is visible in your meeting area)
- Light Refreshments (optional)

NOTE: Discuss the topic of refreshments with Group Members on Week One for their feedback.

THE 1st PROGRAM ORIENTATION MEETING OF YOUR 12-WK SESSION

☐ Arrive 30 minutes before the meeting and arrange furniture comfortably, have supplies on hand, and provide light refreshments if so desired. Ideally, the preferred seating is to have tables so Group Members have ample space to open Study Guides, books, and journals to take notes. And make sure you have enough room to comfortably open your materials, as you will need to page between Member/Leader sections and take notes as well.

Arrival Activity—5-10 minutes
- Greet members as they arrive
- Ask them to make a name tag
- Make sure each member has their own copy of the book and Study Guide (If applicable, collect money for supplies.)

NOTE: You will invariably have couples who want to share study guides and/or books, however it is advised that everyone have their own individual copies of the Study Guide and book. *Making or using photocopies of material is in violation of copyright law.*

Ideally, your group should consist of a maximum of 10-12 people, however you may wish to make exceptions.

☐ Begin the meeting on time and follow the Group Leader Agenda for the Week One Program Orientation on pages 140-142.

Helpful Tools

This Leader Guide has been developed to make it easy for anyone to facilitate a SANITY Support Group, whether or not they have had any experience leading groups.

Therefore, there are instances where specific verbiage has been suggested, as in *"Say this,"* or *"Suggest this,"* or *"Read this"* or *"Ask." These directions will be in italics.* In these instances, feel free to synopsize or elaborate.

I cannot explain all that you may need to do, and I cannot give you directions for handling every situation. However, if God wants to work in the midst of a group, He can and will give you the guidance needed for that time. Your job is to listen for God's voice and trust Him to work through you and through the members of the group.

God has placed you and every Group Member in this place for such a time as this. You can depend on Him to show up and to do amazing things.

God bless you on your new journey!

GROUP LEADER AGENDA
WEEK ONE—PROGRAM ORIENTATION
WELCOME AND WHAT TO EXPECT

Record Start Time

_____

IMPORTANT NOTE:
All sessions are intended
to be 90-minutes total from
the scheduled start time,
not 90-minutes from the time
you actually get started.
Be respectful of everyone's time.

Start your meeting on time. Record start time here. ☞

1. Welcome everyone to the SANITY Support Group:
Share briefly how you came to be a GL, but watch your time.

2. Ask Group Members for self-introductions:
Ask them to briefly share how they learned about this group. Again, watch the time.

3. Open the meeting with your own short prayer:
Follow the guidance of the Holy Spirit, yet be aware not to overwhelm members at first. You may have a melting pot of denominations and various levels of faith. In the future, the meeting will open with a group recitation of the Serenity Prayer.

4. Ask members to identify their individual materials:
Ask them to take a moment to write their name on page one of the Study Guide and on books.

5. Ask everyone to turn to PAGE 8 in this Study Guide:
Say: This week we are going to review pages 8 through 30 in this Study Guide. Allison has specifically asked that some pages be read aloud during this orientation and she encourages us to review all of the pages in this section more carefully in the coming week. Because of the amount of material to review in this session, we won't have open discussions on all of the pages right now. However, future weeks will include more Group Member involvement and feedback. So, let's get started!

PAGE 8—The Six SANITY Steps
Say: Allison encourages us to photocopy this page and put it on our refrigerators & bulletin boards.

PAGE 10—The Faith Component—*Say: Please review this more carefully later.*

PAGE 11—What we'll discover over the next 12-weeks
Ask: Would someone read this list out loud? If no one responds, read it aloud. **Then, continue**.

PAGES 12-13—Meeting Guidelines
Read both pages out loud. Do not ask for a volunteer reader. Do not rush through this.
Ask if there are any questions when you are done reading. **Then, continue.**

PAGE 14—What Finding SANITY is Really All About
Read this page out loud. Do not ask for a volunteer reader.
Say: That's something for us to think about, isn't it? (or something like that) **Then, continue.**

PAGE 15—Get Ready to Live Your Life—*Say: Please review this more carefully later.*

PAGE 16—The Serenity Prayer
Read the text and prayer in the Serenity Prayer box. **Then, move on.**

PAGE 17—Our Mission and the SANITY Support CREED
Say: Literally thousands of people around the world have participated in this 12-week SANITY Support Group for Setting Boundaries® with Your Adult Children. Many of them have indicated that one of the most valuable tools in their ability to eventually set healthy boundaries was the strength they gained from hearing the SANITY Support CREED week-after-week. I will read this aloud today, but in the future we'll ask for **One Group Member** *volunteer to read this aloud at the start of every session.*

Read the CREED aloud, then *Ask: Would anyone like to share what they think or how they feel after hearing this?* (Be prepared for feedback and be careful to watch the clock and keep things moving.) **If no one responds, move on.** Please do not single anyone out to request feedback.

PAGE 18—God Allows U-Turns
Say: This is the title of Allison's first book series. There are 13 volumes in the God Allows U-Turns true short story compilation series. The first four books are now available as ebooks. Visit the website bookstore.

PAGE 19—From Allison's Heart—*Say: Please review this more carefully later.*

PAGES 20-21—A Letter from Abraham Lincoln—*Say: Please review this more carefully later.*

PAGES 22, 23 & 24—Book Review/Quotes/Text Messages—*Say: Please review these later.*

PAGE 25—Weekly Agenda—Review the timeframe format that will be used for every meeting.
Say: This is how every session will be conducted. Allison thinks it's important to be respectful of everyone's time and do our best to keep on track during the sessions.
Ask for group feedback on how/if to have refreshments, and if they prefer 90 min. or 2-hr group?

PAGE 26—God Has a Plan for Your Life—*Say: Please review this more carefully later.*

PAGE 27—SANITY Support Member Covenant Agreement
Say: The "A" Step in SANITY is to ASSEMBLE Supportive People, and Allison thinks it's important that SANITY Support Group Members are willing to make a commitment to be mutually supportive over the next 12-weeks (and hopefully beyond). I'm going to read this out loud. If you're ready to make a Covenant Agreement with group members, please sign your name. For those who are not ready, please pray about making a decision before the next session.

Read this page out loud. Do not ask for a volunteer reader.
Then, give Group Members a few minutes to complete this before moving on to pages 28-29.
Watch your time.

PAGES 28-29—How do you feel right now?

Say: *DO NOT write anything on page 29, we will complete that page on Week 12, but take a few minutes right now to fill-in-the-blanks on page 28, and be brutally honest with yourself.*

Give Group Members a few minutes to complete this before moving on.

PAGE 30—Goals and Closing Prayer

Say: *A "GOAL PAGE" will appear at the end of every weekly session and will include the reading and writing assignments for the coming week. Our goal is to complete the reading and writing assignments BEFORE THE NEXT WEEK'S MEETING. This week is the most reading homework we'll ever have in one week, and it's important for all of us to be on the same page when we next meet, so please do your best to carve out the time needed to complete this week's assignment.*

Say: *Additionally, Allison has asked that everyone begin keeping a SANITY Journal as we proceed. This can be a simple spiral notebook or a bound journal, whatever works best for you. You can also use this SANITY Journal for keeping notes during weekly sessions, and to begin recording your own goals, dreams, and visions.*

Time Check: If there is time remaining in your session you can invite member feedback and encourage group interaction. Also, share information in text box below.

PAGE 30—Closing Prayer

Thank members for attending, invite them back, and confirm date, time and location of your next meeting. *Ask*: if anyone would like to read the **Closing Prayer. If no one volunteers, read aloud.**

Adjourn Meeting and record the time your meeting actually ended: _____

A note from Allison about adding new members to your group:

(Share this with Group Members if there is time.)

Experience proves that when SANITY Support Groups begin meeting, new members will invariably appear—often desperate to join. Especially when they begin to see the SANITY success that Group Members are having. However, the ability to develop a strong and trusting bond among Group Members is based on sharing experiences and personal growth within the group dynamic. That is why I discourage the addition of new Group Members after Week Two. Therefore, if anyone knows of someone who may benefit from this group, please encourage them to purchase their materials ASAP and invite them to attend next week. New members will have to catch up and review Week One Program Orientation information on their own.

LEADER NOTES

Group Session Week 2

GOALS FOR THIS SESSION

This week Group Members will learn:
1. This 12-week session will be a life-changing experience.
2. The difference between positively helping and negatively enabling.
3. If we are an enabler.

Before the Session

☐ **Complete** all of the reading and writing assignments in your own copy of the Study Guide.

☐ **Pray** for guidance as you prepare for this session. Ask God to give you wisdom and discernment as you facilitate this group and as you walk your own **SANITY** journey. Pray for each member of your group.

☐ **Prepare** for any assigned activities, and assemble supplies and materials for next session.

☐ **Record** what God is impressing on your heart and spirit in your SANITY Journal.

Session Day

☐ **Arrive** 30-min. early & set-up room.
☐ **Greet** members as they arrive and remember as the Group Leader, it is your responsibility to start and end on time.

Instruct Group:
Open Study Guide to Page 32

☐ **Step One — Open Meeting (5 min.)**

  ☐ **Remind** members to silence cell phones. **Say:** *Let's prepare our hearts and spirits…*
  ☐ **Group Reading:** Serenity Prayer (pg 16)
  ☐ **Ask** for a volunteer to read the SANITY Support CREED aloud (**pg 17**).

☐ **Step Two — Group Discussion (30 min.)**
How was your week?

☐ **Step Three — Group Discussion (40 min.)**
  Fill-in-the-Blanks. Go through each numeric point, (answer key at end of Study Guide.)
ALSO: See **Leader Prompts** on right

☐ **Step Four — Identify Action Items (10 min.)**
Ask members to identify and share their main goal for this week. (To be discussed next week in **Step Two**.)

IF TIME PERMITS: Review Additional Pages
Listed on the page with the clock graphic

☐ **Step Five — Homework (3 min.)**
Review *What's in Store for Next Week*

☐ **Step Six — Closing Prayer**
Ask for a volunteer to read *Closing Prayer*.

ADJOURN MEETING at 90-minutes

As a Group Leader, you need to be sensitive to what may be happening during sessions if members are deeply moved by something. Look for opportunities to praise and thank the Lord as He begins to convict members of changes they need to make.

Remember, Group Leaders are not counselors or therapists. If you sense someone needs additional help immediately, feel free to stop and pray within the group environment. You can also gently direct them to the top of page 101 in the Study Guide. Be careful not to enable someone who is an enabler—it can be a vicious cycle. (In the event you <u>are</u> a licensed professional, feel free to follow your professional standards for reaching out privately to individuals.)

DURING SESSION: Ask questions like:
- *What was most insightful this week?*
- *What unexpected lesson did you learn?*
- *How is the Lord speaking to you through this particular lesson?*

Leader Prompts for Week

☐ Visit our Facebook Page before the next meeting if you can. Review page 38 and encourage GM's to participate in the SANITY Support Facebook community. This Facebook community is specifically for SANITY Support group members and Setting Boundaries readers....it's a way to stay in touch and share common concerns, triumphs, and SANITY!

Note: If possible, please post something on our Facebook Page yourself, but nothing member specific, remember our CONFIDENTIALITY promise. **The more active you and your group are on our FB page, the more inspiring you can be to others.**

After the Session Self-Evaluation

☐ **Ask** yourself the following questions and jot notes in the spaces below, or in your SANITY Journal:

- How well did I do to begin & end on time?

- What spiritual or mental preparation do I need to make for the next session that may have been lacking this week?

- How can I encourage all members to participate?

- Was there a time I could have responded differently to the needs of Group Members?

- Did I listen to and follow the Leadership of the Holy Spirit?

☐ **Ask** yourself if there are any members who seem to be in crisis mode this week?
   ☐ **Yes** ☐ **No** ☐ **Uncertain**

NOTE: *If yes, pray specifically for them and ask for Holy Spirit wisdom and guidance regarding how to proceed.*

☐ **Read** the **GOALS FOR THIS SESSION** on the following page to get an idea of the preparation required for next week.

☐ **Write** in your SANITY Journal (or below) specific ways you can pray intentionally for Group Members.

Additional Notes From This Week:

Group Session Week 3

GOALS FOR THIS SESSION

This week Group Members will learn:
1. The Six Steps to SANITY
2. The need to STOP the INSANITY
3. What needs to be released in order to begin the journey to SANITY

Before the Session

☐ **Complete** all of the reading and writing assignments in your own copy of the Study Guide.

☐ **Pray** for guidance as you prepare for this session. Ask God to give you wisdom and discernment as you facilitate this group and as you walk your own **SANITY** journey. Pray for each member of your group.

☐ **Prepare** for any assigned activities, and assemble supplies and materials for next session.

☐ **Record** what God is impressing on your heart and spirit in your SANITY Journal.

Session Day

☐ **Arrive** 30-min. early & set-up room.
☐ **Greet** members as they arrive and remember as the Group Leader, it is your responsibility to start and end on time.

Instruct Group:
Open Study Guide to Page 42

☐ **Step One—Open Meeting (5 min.)**

  ☐ **Remind** members to silence cell phones.
    Say: *Let's prepare our hearts and spirits…*
  ☐ **Group Reading:** Serenity Prayer (pg 16)
  ☐ **Ask** for a volunteer to read the SANITY Support CREED aloud (**pg 17**).

☐ **Step Two—Group Discussion (30 min.)**
How was your week?

☐ **Step Three—Group Discussion (40 min.)**
  Fill-in-the-Blanks. Go through each numeric point, (answer key at end of Study Guide.)
ALSO: See **Leader Prompts** on right

☐ **Step Four —Identify Action Items (10 min.)**
Ask members to identify and share their main goal for this week. (To be discussed next week in **Step Two**.)

IF TIME PERMITS: Review Additional Pages
Listed on the page with the clock graphic

☐ **Step Five—Homework (3 min.)**
Review *What's in Store for Next Week*

☐ **Step Six—Closing Prayer**
Ask for a volunteer to read *Closing Prayer*.

ADJOURN MEETING at 90-minutes

There will be a special "Release Celebration" at today's session. When your group gets to Step Four, hand out the slips of paper you have prepared and place the basket in a central location. Ask Group Members to check the boxes that apply, fold the paper in half, and then get up and walk to the basket and drop it in.

DO NOT pass the basket around. A key aspect of this exercise is for Group Members to get up and intentionally release these negative feelings.

Retrieve the basket and read aloud the feelings Group Members are "Releasing." Thank and praise God for His love and guidance to keep us strong on the journey.

DURING SESSION: Ask questions like:

- *What was most insightful this week?*
- *What unexpected lesson did you learn?*
- *How is the Lord speaking to you through this particular lesson?*

Leader Prompts for Week

GROUP LEADER EXERCISE

☐ Photocopy the form on page 172 of this Study Guide and cut into squares.

☐ Bring a bowl/basket to class this week and place in a prominent and accessible place.

☐ Distribute slips of paper to GM's and ask them to complete the form, fold it in half and drop it into the basket/bowl. **NO NAMES**

☐ Read aloud the negative feelings that GM's are "Releasing." Thank and praise God! <u>**SAVE THESE SLIPS**</u> for another exercise in a later week.

☐ Encourage GM's to record their *"Items of Release"* in their SANITY Journals.

After the Session Self-Evaluation

☐ **Ask** yourself the following questions and jot notes in the spaces below, or in your SANITY Journal:

- How well did I do to begin & end on time?

- What spiritual or mental preparation do I need to make for the next session that may have been lacking this week?

- How can I encourage all members to participate?

- Was there a time I could have responded differently to the needs of Group Members?

- Did I listen to and follow the Leadership of the Holy Spirit?

☐ **Ask** yourself if there are any members who seem to be in crisis mode this week?
☐ Yes ☐ No ☐ Uncertain

NOTE: *If yes, pray specifically for them and ask for Holy Spirit wisdom and guidance regarding how to proceed.*

☐ **Read** the **GOALS FOR THIS SESSION** on the following page to get an idea of the preparation required for next week.

☐ **Write** in your SANITY Journal (or below) specific ways you can pray intentionally for Group Members.

Additional Notes From This Week:

Group Session Week 4

GOALS FOR THIS SESSION

This week Group Members will learn:
1. The "S" Step in SANITY
2. Nothing new can START until we learn how to STOP
3. The value of learning HOW and WHAT to STOP

Before the Session

☐ **Complete** all of the reading and writing assignments in your own copy of the Study Guide.

☐ **Pray** for guidance as you prepare for this session. Ask God to give you wisdom and discernment as you facilitate this group and as you walk your own **SANITY** journey. Pray for each member of your group.

☐ **Prepare** for any assigned activities, and assemble supplies and materials for next session.

☐ **Record** what God is impressing on your heart and spirit in your SANITY Journal.

Session Day

☐ **Arrive** 30-min. early & set-up room.
☐ **Greet** members as they arrive and remember as the Group Leader, it is your responsibility to start and end on time.

Instruct Group:
Open Study Guide to Page 50

☐ **Step One—Open Meeting (5 min.)**

  ☐ **Remind** members to silence cell phones.
  Say: *Let's prepare our hearts and spirits…*
  ☐ **Group Reading:** Serenity Prayer (pg 16)
  ☐ **Ask** for a volunteer to read the SANITY Support CREED aloud **(pg 17)**.

☐ **Step Two—Group Discussion (30 min.)**
How was your week?

☐ **Step Three—Group Discussion (40 min.)**
  Fill-in-the-Blanks. Go through each numeric point, (answer key at end of Study Guide.)
ALSO: See **Leader Prompts** on right

☐ **Step Four —Identify Action Items (10 min.)**
Ask members to identify and share their main goal for this week. (To be discussed next week in **Step Two**.)

IF TIME PERMITS: Review Additional Pages
Listed on the page with the clock graphic

☐ **Step Five—Homework (3 min.)**
Review *What's in Store for Next Week*

☐ **Step Six—Closing Prayer**
Ask for a volunteer to read *Closing Prayer*.

ADJOURN MEETING at 90-minutes

Leader Prompts for Week

☐ Take time to discuss the *Things to Stop* list on page 55 and *How We Can Stop* list on page 54. Encourage GM's to photocopy these pages and keep them nearby for easy reference.

☐ Visit our Facebook Page and post something.

☐ **Ask** if anyone visited the **SANITY Support Facebook community** in the past week. Share with your Group Members that I (Allison) often conduct live SKYPE calls with groups (especially groups who are particularly active on our Facebook Page.) Challenge your group to visit FB this week. Then, send me an email to see about setting up a SURPRISE Skype call w/ your group (on a laptop/notebook) at a future meeting. **Allison@AllisonBottke.com**

LEADER PROMPTS: **Ask** questions like:

- *What was most insightful this week?*
- *What unexpected lesson did you learn?*
- *How is the Lord speaking to you through this particular lesson?*

After the Session Self-Evaluation

☐ **Ask** yourself the following questions and jot notes in the spaces below, or in your SANITY Journal:

- How well did I do to begin & end on time?

- What spiritual or mental preparation do I need to make for the next session that may have been lacking this week?

- How can I encourage all members to participate?

- Was there a time I could have responded differently to the needs of Group Members?

- Did I listen to and follow the Leadership of the Holy Spirit?

☐ **Ask** yourself if there are any members who seem to be in crisis mode this week?
☐ **Yes** ☐ **No** ☐ **Uncertain**

NOTE: *If yes, pray specifically for them and ask for Holy Spirit wisdom and guidance regarding how to proceed.*

☐ **Read** the **GOALS FOR THIS SESSION** on the following page to get an idea of the preparation required for next week.

☐ **Write** in your SANITY Journal (or below) specific ways you can pray intentionally for Group Members.

Additional Notes From This Week:

The Beginning

Let's get a jump start on
ACTION PLAN DEVELOPMENT

Never underestimate the power of a written plan

Leader Prompts

Ask someone to read the text box on page 61: **As We Approach Week Six...** Then, ask for Group Member feedback.

Move down to the bottom of page 61 and ask GM's what goes through their minds when they hear this definition and see the gerbil on his wheel. Ask if anyone has ever felt this way, and if so, are they ready to STOP?

Ask GM's to turn the page in their Study Guide and use your Leader Prompts on the next page (page 153) to discuss the **Four Steps to Get Jump Started on Your Action Plan** (Watch your time).

Ask GM's what they think about actually developing a written Action Plan. Jot some comments below (or in your SANITY Journal) to revisit during wks. 7 & 10.

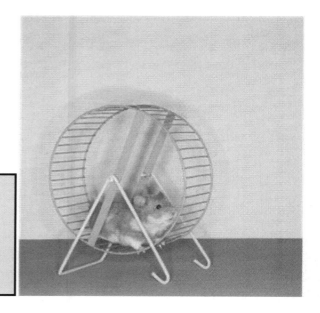

Remember the Definition of INSANITY...
Repeating the same behavior and expecting different results!

GUIDELINES TO DEVELOPING YOUR ACTION PLAN
FOUR STEPS TO GETTING JUMP STARTED

PAGES 62-63 IN STUDY GUIDE

Leader Prompts

Briefly discuss pages 62-63 and encourage GM's *not* to be overwhelmed by this step.
Pay special attention to discussing **Step Four on page 62**. Ask GM's how this particular step can make a difference in the process of developing their Action Plan.

Page 64 in Study Guide
Stop Putting Your Life on Hold!

Leader Prompts

<u>Say this</u>: *Discovering who we are as individuals is a critical part in setting healthy boundaries in any area of life.*

Take time to let your group members discuss what this page means to them. Encourage them to share their own goals and dreams—goals and dreams they have as individuals for their own lives—goals and dreams that do not include issues surrounding their adult children.

Group Session Week 5

GOALS FOR THIS SESSION

This week Group Members will learn:
1. The "A" Step in SANITY
2. We are not alone
3. The value of vulnerability and transparency

Before the Session

☐ **Complete** all of the reading and writing assignments in your own copy of the Study Guide.

☐ **Pray** for guidance as you prepare for this session. Ask God to give you wisdom and discernment as you facilitate this group and as you walk your own **SANITY** journey. Pray for each member of your group.

☐ **Prepare** for any assigned activities, and assemble supplies and materials for next session.

☐ **Record** what God is impressing on your heart and spirit in your SANITY Journal.

Session Day

☐ **Arrive** 30-min. early & set-up room.
☐ **Greet** members as they arrive and remember as the Group Leader, it is your responsibility to start and end on time.

Instruct Group:
Open Study Guide to Page 58

☐ **Step One—Open Meeting** (5 min.)

☐ **Remind** members to silence cell phones.
   Say: *Let's prepare our hearts and spirits…*
☐ **Group Reading:** Serenity Prayer (pg 16)
☐ **Ask** for a volunteer to read the SANITY Support CREED aloud (**pg 17**).

☐ **Step Two—Group Discussion** (30 min.)
How was your week?

☐ **Step Three—Group Discussion** (40 min.)
   Fill-in-the-Blanks. Go through each numeric point, (answer key at end of Study Guide.)
ALSO: See **Leader Prompts** on right

☐ **Step Four —Identify Action Items** (10 min.)
Ask members to identify and share their main goal for this week. (To be discussed next week in **Step Two**.)

IF TIME PERMITS: Review Additional Pages
Listed on the page with the clock graphic

☐ **Step Five—Homework** (3 min.)
Review *What's in Store for Next Week*

☐ **Step Six—Closing Prayer**
Ask for a volunteer to read *Closing Prayer*.

ADJOURN MEETING at 90-minutes

Remember, as a Group Leader, you need to be sensitive to what may be happening during sessions if members are deeply moved by something. Look for opportunities to praise and thank the Lord as He begins to convict members of changes they need to make.

Remember, Group Leaders are not counselors or therapists. If you sense someone needs additional help immediately, feel free to stop and pray within the group environment. You can also gently direct them to the top of page 101 in the Study Guide. Be careful not to enable someone who is an enabler—it can be a vicious cycle. (In the event you <u>are</u> a licensed professional, feel free to follow your professional standards for reaching out to individuals.)

DURING SESSION: Ask questions like:
- *What was most insightful this week?*
- *What unexpected lesson did you learn?*
- *How is the Lord speaking to you through this particular lesson?*

Leader Prompts for Week

DO NOT spend the full 40-minutes on Step Three this week, move quickly through pages 58-59 and plan to spend more time discussing the *"Jump Start Assignment"* on pages 61-63.

See your Leader Guide pages 152-153!

It would be a really great thing if you could develop your 3-ring binder before the meeting and take it to show as an example. Feel free to send me an email if you have questions about this.

<u>Allison@AllisonBottke.com</u>

After the Session Self-Evaluation

☐ **Ask** yourself the following questions and jot notes in the spaces below, or in your SANITY Journal:

- How well did I do to begin & end on time?

- What spiritual or mental preparation do I need to make for the next session that may have been lacking this week?

- How can I encourage all members to participate?

- Was there a time I could have responded differently to the needs of Group Members?

- Did I listen to and follow the Leadership of the Holy Spirit?

☐ **Ask** yourself if there are any members who seem to be in crisis mode this week?
    ☐ **Yes**   ☐ **No**   ☐ **Uncertain**

NOTE: *If yes, pray specifically for them and ask for Holy Spirit wisdom and guidance regarding how to proceed.*

☐ **Read** the **GOALS FOR THIS SESSION** on the following page to get an idea of the preparation required for next week.

☐ **Write** in your SANITY Journal (or below) specific ways you can pray intentionally for Group Members.

Additional Notes From This Week:

Group Session Week 6

GOALS FOR THIS SESSION

This week Group Members will learn:
1. The "N" Step in SANITY
2. What an excuse really is
3. Why Barney Fife was a brilliant man

Before the Session

☐ **Complete** all of the reading and writing assignments in your own copy of the Study Guide.

☐ **Pray** for guidance as you prepare for this session. Ask God to give you wisdom and discernment as you facilitate this group and as you walk your own **SANITY** journey. Pray for each member of your group.

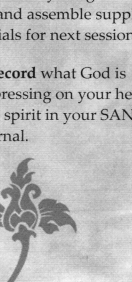

☐ **Prepare** for any assigned activities, and assemble supplies and materials for next session.

☐ **Record** what God is impressing on your heart and spirit in your SANITY Journal.

Session Day

☐ **Arrive** 30-min. early & set-up room.
☐ **Greet** members as they arrive and remember as the Group Leader, it is your responsibility to start and end on time.

Instruct Group:
Open Study Guide to Page 68

☐ **Step One—Open Meeting (5 min.)**

   ☐ **Remind** members to silence cell phones. **Say:** *Let's prepare our hearts and spirits…*
   ☐ **Group Reading:** Serenity Prayer (pg 16)
   ☐ **Ask** for a volunteer to read the SANITY Support CREED aloud **(pg 17)**.

☐ **Step Two—Group Discussion (30 min.)**
How was your week?

☐ **Step Three—Group Discussion (40 min.)**
   Fill-in-the-Blanks. Go through each numeric point, (answer key at end of Study Guide.)
ALSO: See **Leader Prompts** on right

☐ **Step Four —Identify Action Items (10 min.)**
Ask members to identify and share their main goal for this week. (To be discussed next week in **Step Two**.)

IF TIME PERMITS: Review Additional Pages
Listed on the page with the clock graphic

☐ **Step Five—Homework (3 min.)**
Review *What's in Store for Next Week*

☐ **Step Six—Closing Prayer**
Ask for a volunteer to read *Closing Prayer*.

ADJOURN MEETING at 90-minutes

SCRIPTURE STRENGTH

Whether you turn to the right or to the left, your ears will hear a voice behind you, saying, "This is the way; walk in it."

Isaiah 30:21 (NIV)

DURING SESSION: Ask questions like:

- *What was most insightful this week?*
- *What unexpected lesson did you learn?*
- *How is the Lord speaking to you through this particular lesson?*

Leader Prompts for Week

Turn to page 124 in the book and have someone read the last three paragraphs of the chapter, starting with, *"My son was a fallen…"*

Discuss Proverbs 4:23 and page 71 in the Study Guide.

After the Session Self-Evaluation

☐ **Ask** yourself the following questions and jot notes in the spaces below, or in your SANITY Journal:

- How well did I do to begin & end on time?

- What spiritual or mental preparation do I need to make for the next session that may have been lacking this week?

- How can I encourage all members to participate?

- Was there a time I could have responded differently to the needs of Group Members?

- Did I listen to and follow the Leadership of the Holy Spirit?

☐ **Ask** yourself if there are any members who seem to be in crisis mode this week?
☐ **Yes** ☐ **No** ☐ **Uncertain**

NOTE: *If yes, pray specifically for them and ask for Holy Spirit wisdom and guidance regarding how to proceed.*

☐ **Read** the **GOALS FOR THIS SESSION** on the following page to get an idea of the preparation required for next week.

☐ **Write** in your SANITY Journal (or below) specific ways you can pray intentionally for Group Members.

Additional Notes From This Week:

Group Session Week 7

GOALS FOR THIS SESSION

This week Group Members will learn:
1. The "I" Step in INSANITY
2. The time-honored value of "putting it in writing"
3. How to clearly articulate expectations in order to avoid assumptions

Before the Session

☐ **Complete** all of the reading and writing assignments in your own copy of the Study Guide.

☐ **Pray** for guidance as you prepare for this session. Ask God to give you wisdom and discernment as you facilitate this group and as you walk your own **SANITY** journey. Pray for each member of your group.

☐ **Prepare** for any assigned activities, and assemble supplies and materials for next session.

☐ **Record** what God is impressing on your heart and spirit in your SANITY Journal.

Session Day

☐ **Arrive** 30-min. early & set-up room.
☐ **Greet** members as they arrive and remember as the Group Leader, it is your responsibility to start and end on time.

Instruct Group:
Open Study Guide to Page 76

☐ **Step One—Open Meeting (5 min.)**

☐ **Remind** members to silence cell phones.
Say: *Let's prepare our hearts and spirits…*
☐ **Group Reading:** Serenity Prayer (pg 16)
☐ **Ask** for a volunteer to read the SANITY Support CREED aloud **(pg 17)**.

☐ **Step Two—Group Discussion (30 min.)**
How was your week?

☐ **Step Three—Group Discussion (40 min.)**
Fill-in-the-Blanks. Go through each numeric point, (answer key at end of Study Guide.)
ALSO: See **Leader Prompts** on right

☐ **Step Four —Identify Action Items (10 min.)**
Ask members to identify and share their main goal for this week. (To be discussed next week in **Step Two**.)

IF TIME PERMITS: Review Additional Pages
Listed on the page with the clock graphic

☐ **Step Five—Homework (3 min.)**
Review *What's in Store for Next Week*

☐ **Step Six—Closing Prayer**
Ask for a volunteer to read *Closing Prayer*.

ADJOURN MEETING at 90-minutes

As a Group Leader, you need to be sensitive to what may be happening during sessions if members are deeply moved by something. Look for opportunities to praise and thank the Lord as He begins to convict members of changes they need to make.

Remember, Group Leaders are not counselors or therapists. If you sense someone needs additional help immediately, feel free to stop and pray within the group environment. You can also gently direct them to the top of page 101 in the Study Guide. Be careful not to enable someone who is an enabler—it can be a vicious cycle. (In the event you <u>are</u> a licensed professional, feel free to follow your professional standards for reaching out to individuals.)

DURING SESSION: Ask questions like:

- *What was most insightful this week?*
- *What unexpected lesson did you learn?*
- *How is the Lord speaking to you through this particular lesson?*

Leader Prompts for Week

Step Three: Move quickly through the fill-in-the-blank assignment on pages 76-77 and spend time reviewing and discussing pages 80-81 of the Study Guide.

Ask GM's if they are working on their 3-ring binders for their Action Plan.

Read the section of text on page 134 from Cecil Murphey.

Ask GM's what it would look like to teach **IN**dependence (as opposed to **DE**pendence.)

After the Session Self-Evaluation

☐ **Ask** yourself the following questions and jot notes in the spaces below, or in your SANITY Journal:

- How well did I do to begin & end on time?

- What spiritual or mental preparation do I need to make for the next session that may have been lacking this week?

- How can I encourage all members to participate?

- Was there a time I could have responded differently to the needs of Group Members?

- Did I listen to and follow the Leadership of the Holy Spirit?

☐ **Ask** yourself if there are any members who seem to be in crisis mode this week?

☐ **Yes** ☐ **No** ☐ **Uncertain**

NOTE: *If yes, pray specifically for them and ask for Holy Spirit wisdom and guidance regarding how to proceed.*

☐ **Read** the **GOALS FOR THIS SESSION** on the following page to get an idea of the preparation required for next week.

☐ **Write** in your SANITY Journal (or below) specific ways you can pray intentionally for Group Members.

Additional Notes From This Week:

Group Session Week 8

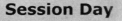

GOALS FOR THIS SESSION

This week Group Members will learn:
1. The "T" Step in SANITY
2. Why it's so hard to trust
3. How God speaks to us

Before the Session

☐ **Complete** all of the reading and writing assignments in your own copy of the Study Guide.

☐ **Pray** for guidance as you prepare for this session. Ask God to give you wisdom and discernment as you facilitate this group and as you walk your own **SANITY** journey. Pray for each member of your group.

☐ **Prepare** for any assigned activities, and assemble supplies and materials for next session.

☐ **Record** what God is impressing on your heart and spirit in your SANITY Journal.

Session Day

☐ **Arrive** 30-min. early & set-up room.
☐ **Greet** members as they arrive and remember as the Group Leader, it is your responsibility to start and end on time.

Instruct Group:
Open Study Guide to Page 84

☐ **Step One—Open Meeting** (5 min.)

　☐ **Remind** members to silence cell phones.
　　Say: *Let's prepare our hearts and spirits...*
　☐ **Group Reading:** Serenity Prayer (pg 16)
　☐ **Ask** for a volunteer to read the SANITY Support CREED aloud (**pg 17**).

☐ **Step Two—Group Discussion** (30 min.)
How was your week?

☐ **Step Three—Group Discussion** (40 min.)
Fill-in-the-Blanks. Go through each numeric point, (answer key at end of Study Guide.)
ALSO: See **Leader Prompts** on right

☐ **Step Four —Identify Action Items** (10 min.)
Ask members to identify and share their main goal for this week. (To be discussed next week in **Step Two**.)

IF TIME PERMITS: Review Additional Pages
Listed on the page with the clock graphic

☐ **Step Five—Homework** (3 min.)
Review *What's in Store for Next Week*

☐ **Step Six—Closing Prayer**
Ask for a volunteer to read *Closing Prayer*.

ADJOURN MEETING at 90-minutes

As a Group Leader, you need to be sensitive to what may be happening during sessions if members are deeply moved by something. Look for opportunities to praise and thank the Lord as He begins to convict members of changes they need to make.

Remember, Group Leaders are not counselors or therapists. If you sense someone needs additional help immediately, feel free to stop and pray within the group environment. You can also gently direct them to the top of page 101 in the Study Guide. Be careful not to enable someone who is an enabler—it can be a vicious cycle. (In the event you are a licensed professional, feel free to follow your professional standards for reaching out to individuals.)

DURING SESSION: Ask questions like:

- *What was most insightful this week?*
- *What unexpected lesson did you learn?*
- *How is the Lord speaking to you through this particular lesson?*

Leader Prompts for Week

Step Three: Ask GM's to share their responses to question #6 on page 85 of Study Guide.

Discuss what it means to ask for Holy Spirit wisdom and discernment in addressing our concerns.

After the Session Self-Evaluation

☐ **Ask** yourself the following questions and jot notes in the spaces below, or in your SANITY Journal:

- How well did I do to begin & end on time?

- What spiritual or mental preparation do I need to make for the next session that may have been lacking this week?

- How can I encourage all members to participate?

- Was there a time I could have responded differently to the needs of Group Members?

- Did I listen to and follow the Leadership of the Holy Spirit?

☐ **Ask** yourself if there are any members who seem to be in crisis mode this week?
　　　☐ **Yes** ☐ **No** ☐ **Uncertain**

NOTE: *If yes, pray specifically for them and ask for Holy Spirit wisdom and guidance regarding how to proceed.*

☐ **Read** the **GOALS FOR THIS SESSION** on the following page to get an idea of the preparation required for next week.

☐ **Write** in your SANITY Journal (or below) specific ways you can pray intentionally for Group Members.

Additional Notes From This Week:

Group Session Week 9

GOALS FOR THIS SESSION

This week Group Members will learn:
1. The "Y" Step in SANITY
2. We are not in control
3. We are at our strongest when we yield

Before the Session

☐ **Complete** all of the reading and writing assignments in your own copy of the Study Guide.

☐ **Pray** for guidance as you prepare for this session. Ask God to give you wisdom and discernment as you facilitate this group and as you walk your own **SANITY** journey. Pray for each member of your group.

☐ **Prepare** for any assigned activities, and assemble supplies and materials for next session.

☐ **Record** what God is impressing on your heart and spirit in your SANITY Journal.

Session Day

☐ **Arrive** 30-min. early & set-up room.
☐ **Greet** members as they arrive and remember as the Group Leader, it is your responsibility to start and end on time.

Instruct Group:
Open Study Guide to Page 88

☐ **Step One—Open Meeting (5 min.)**

  ☐ **Remind** members to silence cell phones.
  Say: *Let's prepare our hearts and spirits…*
  ☐ **Group Reading:** Serenity Prayer (pg 16)
  ☐ **Ask** for a volunteer to read the SANITY Support CREED aloud (**pg 17**).

☐ **Step Two—Group Discussion (30 min.)**
How was your week?

☐ **Step Three—Group Discussion (40 min.)**
  Fill-in-the-Blanks. Go through each numeric point, (answer key at end of Study Guide.)
ALSO: See **Leader Prompts** on right

☐ **Step Four —Identify Action Items (10 min.)**
Ask members to identify and share their main goal for this week. (To be discussed next week in **Step Two**.)

IF TIME PERMITS: Review Additional Pages
Listed on the page with the clock graphic

☐ **Step Five—Homework (3 min.)**
Review *What's in Store for Next Week*

☐ **Step Six—Closing Prayer**
Ask for a volunteer to read *Closing Prayer*.

ADJOURN MEETING at 90-minutes

As a Group Leader, you need to be sensitive to what may be happening during sessions if members are deeply moved by something. Look for opportunities to praise and thank the Lord as He begins to convict members of changes they need to make.

Remember, Group Leaders are not counselors or therapists. If you sense someone needs additional help immediately, feel free to stop and pray within the group environment. You can also gently direct them to the top of page 101 in the Study Guide. Be careful not to enable someone who is an enabler—it can be a vicious cycle. (In the event you <u>are</u> a licensed professional, feel free to follow your professional standards for reaching out to individuals.)

DURING SESSION: Ask questions like:

- *What was most insightful this week?*
- *What unexpected lesson did you learn?*
- *How is the Lord speaking to you through this particular lesson?*

Leader Prompts for Week

Step Three: Spend time talking about what "Yield" means to group members.

Discuss Allison's letter on pages 92-93 of Study Guide. If you have time, perhaps someone could read this aloud.

After the Session Self-Evaluation

☐ **Ask** yourself the following questions and jot notes in the spaces below, or in your SANITY Journal:

- How well did I do to begin & end on time?

- What spiritual or mental preparation do I need to make for the next session that may have been lacking this week?

- How can I encourage all members to participate?

- Was there a time I could have responded differently to the needs of Group Members?

- Did I listen to and follow the Leadership of the Holy Spirit?

☐ **Ask** yourself if there are any members who seem to be in crisis mode this week?
  ☐ **Yes** ☐ **No** ☐ **Uncertain**

NOTE: *If yes, pray specifically for them and ask for Holy Spirit wisdom and guidance regarding how to proceed.*

☐ **Read** the **GOALS FOR THIS SESSION** on the following page to get an idea of the preparation required for next week.

☐ **Write** in your SANITY Journal (or below) specific ways you can pray intentionally for Group Members.

Additional Notes From This Week:

Group Session Week 10

GOALS FOR THIS SESSION

This week Group Members will learn:
1. The power of a written plan
2. The healing properties of a written plan
3. The freedom of a written plan

Before the Session

☐ **Complete** all of the reading and writing assignments in your own copy of the Study Guide.

☐ **Pray** for guidance as you prepare for this session. Ask God to give you wisdom and discernment as you facilitate this group and as you walk your own **SANITY** journey. Pray for each member of your group.

☐ **Prepare** for any assigned activities, and assemble supplies and materials for next session.

☐ **Record** what God is impressing on your heart and spirit in your SANITY Journal.

Session Day

☐ **Arrive** 30-min. early & set-up room.
☐ **Greet** members as they arrive and remember as the Group Leader, it is your responsibility to start and end on time.

Instruct Group:
Open Study Guide to Page 96

☐ **Step One—Open Meeting (5 min.)**

  ☐ **Remind** members to silence cell phones.
    Say: *Let's prepare our hearts and spirits…*
  ☐ **Group Reading:** Serenity Prayer (pg 16)
  ☐ **Ask** for a volunteer to read the SANITY Support CREED aloud (**pg 17**).

☐ **Step Two—Group Discussion (30 min.)**
How was your week?

☐ **Step Three—Group Discussion (40 min.)**
  Fill-in-the-Blanks. Go through each numeric point, (answer key at end of Study Guide.)
ALSO: See **Leader Prompts** on right

☐ **Step Four —Identify Action Items (10 min.)**
Ask members to identify and share their main goal for this week. (To be discussed next week in **Step Two**.)

IF TIME PERMITS: Review Additional Pages
Listed on the page with the clock graphic

☐ **Step Five—Homework (3 min.)**
Review *What's in Store for Next Week*

☐ **Step Six—Closing Prayer**
Ask for a volunteer to read *Closing Prayer*.

ADJOURN MEETING at 90-minutes

As a Group Leader, you need to be sensitive to what may be happening during sessions if members are deeply moved by something. Look for opportunities to praise and thank the Lord as He begins to convict members of changes they need to make.

Remember, Group Leaders are not counselors or therapists. If you sense someone needs additional help immediately, feel free to stop and pray within the group environment. You can also gently direct them to the top of page 85 in the Study Guide. Be careful not to enable someone who is an enabler—it can be a vicious cycle. (In the event you <u>are</u> a licensed professional, feel free to follow your professional standards for reaching out to individuals.)

DURING SESSION: Ask questions like:

- *What was most insightful this week?*
- *What unexpected lesson did you learn?*
- *How is the Lord speaking to you through this particular lesson?*

Leader Prompts for Week

Step Three: Take a few minutes to discuss the *"Personal Note from Allison"* on page 100. Be sensitive about this topic—especially if someone opens up to share about a marriage in trouble.

Then, encourage GM's to discuss how their written plans are progressing.

Invariably, there are often Group Members who find it very difficult to put any type of Action Plan in writing, and this often becomes frustrating for Group Leaders. Ask the Lord to give you peace about situations like this—and wisdom and discernment for how—and if—you need to address the issue.

After the Session Self-Evaluation

☐ **Ask** yourself the following questions and jot notes in the spaces below, or in your SANITY Journal:

- How well did I do to begin & end on time?

- What spiritual or mental preparation do I need to make for the next session that may have been lacking this week?

- How can I encourage all members to participate?

- Was there a time I could have responded differently to the needs of Group Members?

- Did I listen to and follow the Leadership of the Holy Spirit?

☐ **Ask** yourself if there are any members who seem to be in crisis mode this week?
    ☐ **Yes** ☐ **No** ☐ **Uncertain**

NOTE: *If yes, pray specifically for them and ask for Holy Spirit wisdom and guidance regarding how to proceed.*

☐ **Read** the **GOALS FOR THIS SESSION** on the following page to get an idea of the preparation required for next week.

☐ **Write** in your SANITY Journal (or below) specific ways you can pray intentionally for Group Members.

Additional Notes From This Week:

Group Session Week 11

GOALS FOR THIS SESSION

This week Group Members will learn:
1. The truth about consequences
2. The pain of consequences
3. How to prepare for consequences
4. Make sure to read Leader Prompts and factor in time to discuss these.

Before the Session

☐ **Complete** all of the reading and writing assignments in your own copy of the Study Guide.

☐ **Pray** for guidance as you prepare for this session. Ask God to give you wisdom and discernment as you facilitate this group and as you walk your own **SANITY** journey. Pray for each member of your group.

☐ **Prepare** for any assigned activities, and assemble supplies and materials for next session.

☐ **Record** what God is impressing on your heart and spirit in your SANITY Journal.

Session Day

☐ **Arrive** 30-min. early & set-up room.
☐ **Greet** members as they arrive and remember as the Group Leader, it is your responsibility to start and end on time.

Instruct Group:
Open Study Guide to Page 104

☐ **Step One—Open Meeting (5 min.)**

☐ **Remind** members to silence cell phones.
Say: *Let's prepare our hearts and spirits…*
☐ **Group Reading:** Serenity Prayer (pg 16)
☐ **Ask** for a volunteer to read the SANITY Support CREED aloud **(pg 17)**.

☐ **Step Two—Group Discussion (30 min.)**
How was your week?

☐ **Step Three—Group Discussion (40 min.)**
Fill-in-the-Blanks. Go through each numeric point, (answer key at end of Study Guide.)
ALSO: See **Leader Prompts** on right

☐ **Step Four —Identify Action Items (10 min.)**
Ask members to identify and share their main goal for this week. (To be discussed next week in **Step Two**.)

IF TIME PERMITS: Review Additional Pages
Listed on the page with the clock graphic

☐ **Step Five—Homework (3 min.)**
Review *What's in Store for Next Week*

☐ **Step Six—Closing Prayer**
Ask for a volunteer to read *Closing Prayer*.

ADJOURN MEETING at 90-minutes

Leader Prompts for Week

1. Talk about *Distorted Thinking* when it comes to considering the consequences. Here's an example of distorted thinking:

You refuse to give your son any more cash and he gets arrested for stealing a pack of cigarettes from a convenience store. He blames you for not giving him money and you begin to feel guilty, blaming yourself for what happened. Yet he was arrested as a consequence of a choice he made—*you are not to blame because you made the choice to stop giving him money*. It is *not* your fault. That said, how has distorted thinking about consequences kept us in bondage?

2. Review pages 107 & 108 in Study Guide. Ask for feedback on what resonates with your Group Members concerning this topic of consequences.

3. Ask someone to read aloud the revised **INSANITY CREED** on page 109. Discuss it.

4. Next week will be the final meeting in our twelve-week session, encourage GM's to post on the Facebook SANITY page—sharing what the past eleven weeks has meant to them. Remind them that God can use theiur comments and experiences to help others change their lives.

Make sure to contact Allison and let her know your group is about to end, and give her an update on if you (or someone else) will be conducting another 12-week session.

After the Session Self-Evaluation

☐ **Ask** yourself the following questions and jot notes in the spaces below, or in your SANITY Journal:

- How well did I do to begin & end on time?

- What spiritual or mental preparation do I need to make for the next session that may have been lacking this week?

- How can I encourage all members to participate?

- Was there a time I could have responded differently to the needs of Group Members?

- Did I listen to and follow the Leadership of the Holy Spirit?

☐ **Ask** yourself if there are any members who seem to be in crisis mode this week?
     ☐ Yes ☐ No ☐ Uncertain

NOTE: *If yes, pray specifically for them and ask for Holy Spirit wisdom and guidance regarding how to proceed.*

☐ **Read** the **GOALS FOR THIS SESSION** on the following page to get an idea of the preparation required for next week.

☐ **Write** in your SANITY Journal (or below) specific ways you can pray intentionally for Group Members.

Additional Notes From This Week:

Group Session Week 12

GOALS FOR THIS SESSION

This week Group Members will learn:
1. How far we have come
2. It's okay to pursue our own goals and dreams
3. God has a plan for us and for adult children

Before the Session

☐ **Complete** all of the reading and writing assignments in your own copy of the Study Guide.

☐ **Pray** for guidance as you prepare for this session. Ask God to give you wisdom and discernment as you facilitate this group and as you walk your own **SANITY** journey. Pray for each member of your group.

☐ **Prepare** for any assigned activities, and assemble supplies and materials for next session. **PHOTOCOPY PAGE 174 HANDOUT**

☐ **Record** what God is impressing on your heart and spirit in your SANITY Journal.

Session Day

☐ **Arrive** 30-min. early & set-up room.
☐ **Greet** members as they arrive and remember as the Group Leader, it is your responsibility to start and end on time.

Instruct Group:
Open Study Guide to Page 112

☐ **Step One—Open Meeting** (5 min.)

   ☐ **Remind** members to silence cell phones.
     Say: *Let's prepare our hearts and spirits...*
   ☐ **Group Reading:** Serenity Prayer (pg 16)
   ☐ **Ask** for a volunteer to read the SANITY Support CREED aloud (**pg 17**).

☐ **Step Two—Group Discussion** (30 min.)
How was your week?

☐ **Step Three—Group Discussion** (40 min.)
Fill-in-the-Blanks. Go through each numeric point, (answer key at end of Study Guide.)
ALSO: See **Leader Prompts** on right

☐ **Step Four —Identify Action Items** (10 min.)
Ask members to identify and share their main goal for this week. (To be discussed next week in **Step Two**.)

IF TIME PERMITS: Review Additional Pages
Listed on the page with the clock graphic

☐ **Step Five—Homework** (3 min.)
Review *What's in Store for Next Week*

☐ **Step Six—Closing Prayer**
Ask for a volunteer to read *Closing Prayer*.

ADJOURN MEETING at 90-minutes

1. Make photocopies of page 174 and take to group. Collect these at end of the group.
2. Ask GM's to turn to page 29 of SG and take a few minutes to fill-in-the-blanks.
3. Ask GM's to share what they wrote on page 28 on Week One and what they have now written on page 29 in Week Twelve.
4. Spend time talking about what this group has meant to group members, and make plans to stay connected on the Facebook Community page.
5. Distribute Program Evaluation forms and give GM's 5-10 minutes while in class to complete them. **Collect completed forms and mail them directly to Allison at address listed on website Contact page.** (See note below.)

Allison & Christopher, Christmas eve at church in 2011—Fort Worth, TX

A SPECIAL GIFT FOR GROUP LEADERS

When you mail your completed Program Evaluation Forms, make sure to include your entire name and address so Allison can mail you a special Leader Appreciation gift.

Thank you ...

Dear Group Leader,

Thank you for all you have done to lead this SANITY Support Group the past twelve weeks.

I know your leadership has helped to change lives.

May God continue to bless the work of your hands and heart. Please pray about leading another SANITY Support Group and encourage other Group Members to consider doing the same as the need to spread the message of SANITY is great.

God's peace,

Allison

Allison Bottke's
Setting Boundaries Book Series
will help you find ...

S A N I T Y

SANITY *Support*
SIX STEPS TO HOPE AND HEALING

SettingBoundariesBooks.com

HELPFUL LEADER RESOURCES

Check out the following pages to help you be a more effective Group Leader!

Leader Resources

6-Steps to S.A.N.I.T.Y. and 12-Weeks to Freedom
SANITY IS COMING TO YOUR TOWN!

Start Date: _____
Meeting Time: _____
    (All 12 meetings are 90-minutes)
Location: _____
City: _____
Contact: _____
Phone: _____
eMail: _____

REGISTRATION IS FREE
(But group size is limited!)

All Group Members must have a copy of the book and companion study guide. Materials are widely available at bookstores and online.

Setting Boundaries with Your Adult Children

SIX STEPS TO HOPE AND HEALING FOR STRUGGLING PARENTS

ALLISON BOTTKE

SettingBoundariesBooks.com

As you begin your journey on the road to SANITY YOU WILL DISCOVER....

- The difference between positively helping and negatively enabling.
- Why we negatively enable and why we must stop.
- The power of love and forgiveness.
- Love is *not* spelled **M-O-N-E-Y**.
- Sometimes it's a good thing to say *no*.
- Saying no does *not* make us bad parents or grandparents.
- How to identify whose chaos and crisis it really is.
- How to separate our own lives from the lives of our adult children.
- How to develop a Plan-of-Action that works.
- The power of considering the consequences.
- How to be strong *and* loving during turbulent times.
- How to view trials and tribulations as stepping stones to great things.
- The value of yielding everything to God.
- How to love our adult children enough to let them go.
- The joy of what it feels like to *live our own lives*.

SANITY MAKES A COMEBACK!

FOR IMMEDIATE RELEASE

Contact Me: _____

Date: _____

THREE MEDIA OPPORTUNITIES:

*1. Please list this upcoming 12-week workshop in your Community Calendar Section (**Primary Request**)*
2. Consider writing an article/blog about this local SANITY Support Group and/or Group Leader
3. Consider writing an article/blog on the Setting Boundaries® book series and/or author. There are now six books in this bestselling, award winning series from Harvest House Publishers.

Local Group Leader Name: _____
Local Group Leader Telephone: _____
Local Group Leader email: _____

SANITY SUPPORT IS COMING TO TOWN!

City: _____: Do you have an adult child whose choices are breaking your heart? Do you live with chaos, crisis, and drama brought on by the poor choices your adult child is making? If so, you are not alone, this is an epidemic with catastrophic consequences. If you or someone you know is dealing with a difficult relationship with an adult child, help is on the way. **SANITY IS POSSIBLE!** Join the growing network of **SANITY SUPPORT** Groups being conducted worldwide. Begin a **12-WEEK PROGRAM** based on the bestselling book: *SETTING BOUNDARIES WITH YOUR ADULT CHILDREN* written by Allison Bottke. Designed to bring hope and healing to struggling parents and grandparents, <u>6 STEPS TO SANITY AND 12-WEEKS TO FREEDOM</u> will change your life and it's coming to your town! **REGISTER NOW.** There is no fee for the 12-week workshop, but every Group Member needs their own copies of the book and companion study guide. (Materials are widely available at bookstores or online.)

12-Week SANITY Support Session Will Begin:

Day: _____   Date: _____   Time: _____

Location: _____

Address: _____

For more information contact/call: _____

Phone: _____   email: _____

This Week
I Am Releasing...

☐ Guilt ☐ Anger
☐ Fear ☐ Frustration
☐ Hurt ☐ Hopelessness
☐ Feelings of Inadequacy
☐ Worry ☐ Anxiety ☐ Stress
☐ Other: _____

NO NAMES PLEASE

This Week
I Am Releasing...

☐ Guilt ☐ Anger
☐ Fear ☐ Frustration
☐ Hurt ☐ Hopelessness
☐ Feelings of Inadequacy
☐ Worry ☐ Anxiety ☐ Stress
☐ Other: _____

NO NAMES PLEASE

This Week
I Am Releasing...

☐ Guilt ☐ Anger
☐ Fear ☐ Frustration
☐ Hurt ☐ Hopelessness
☐ Feelings of Inadequacy
☐ Worry ☐ Anxiety ☐ Stress
☐ Other: _____

NO NAMES PLEASE

This Week
I Am Releasing...

☐ Guilt ☐ Anger
☐ Fear ☐ Frustration
☐ Hurt ☐ Hopelessness
☐ Feelings of Inadequacy
☐ Worry ☐ Anxiety ☐ Stress
☐ Other: _____

NO NAMES PLEASE

This Week
I Am Releasing...

☐ Guilt ☐ Anger
☐ Fear ☐ Frustration
☐ Hurt ☐ Hopelessness
☐ Feelings of Inadequacy
☐ Worry ☐ Anxiety ☐ Stress
☐ Other: _____

NO NAMES PLEASE

This Week
I Am Releasing...

☐ Guilt ☐ Anger
☐ Fear ☐ Frustration
☐ Hurt ☐ Hopelessness
☐ Feelings of Inadequacy
☐ Worry ☐ Anxiety ☐ Stress
☐ Other: _____

NO NAMES PLEASE

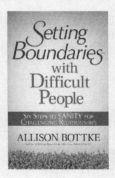

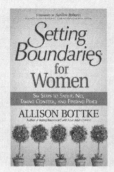

Program Evaluation Form

At *Setting Boundaries Books*, we continually strive to improve our *SANITY Support* programs. Your feedback about the 12-week program you recently attended will assist us with this process.

Program Location: _____

Group Leader: _____

Today's Date: _____

Your Name (Last Name Optional): _____

Email Address: _____

Please indicate your level of satisfaction with each of the following:

Program met my expectations	*poor*	*fair*	*satisfactory*	*good*	*excellent*
Program content	*poor*	*fair*	*satisfactory*	*good*	*excellent*
Ability of Leader to communicate content	*poor*	*fair*	*satisfactory*	*good*	*excellent*
Content and usefulness of Study Guide	*poor*	*fair*	*satisfactory*	*good*	*excellent*
Area in which program was held	*poor*	*fair*	*satisfactory*	*good*	*excellent*
Convenience of program day and time	*poor*	*fair*	*satisfactory*	*good*	*excellent*

If you answered "poor" or "fair" to any of the above please indicate your reasons:
_____

How did you hear about this 12-week program? _____

Would you recommend this program to friends or family?   *Yes   No*
Would you read additional books in the Setting Boundaries series as a result of this program? *Yes   No*

What changes, if any, would you recommend for this program? _____
_____
_____

Additional Comment and/or Endorsement Quote:_____
_____
_____
_____
_____

Thank you for providing your feedback!

ANSWER KEY

NOTES:

Allison **Bottke**

is the award-winning author of the acclaimed *Setting Boundaries*® series and the founder of the SANITY Support Group, an outreach based on the bestselling *Setting Boundaries*® series from Harvest House Publishers. She is also the founder and general editor of more than a dozen volumes in the popular *God Allows U-Turns*® anthology. She has written or edited more than 30 non-fiction and fiction books and is a frequent guest on national radio and TV programs. Allison also has a passion to help writers achieve their dreams, and she has served on the faculty at many national writing conferences. Allison lives in the Dallas/Fort Worth area.

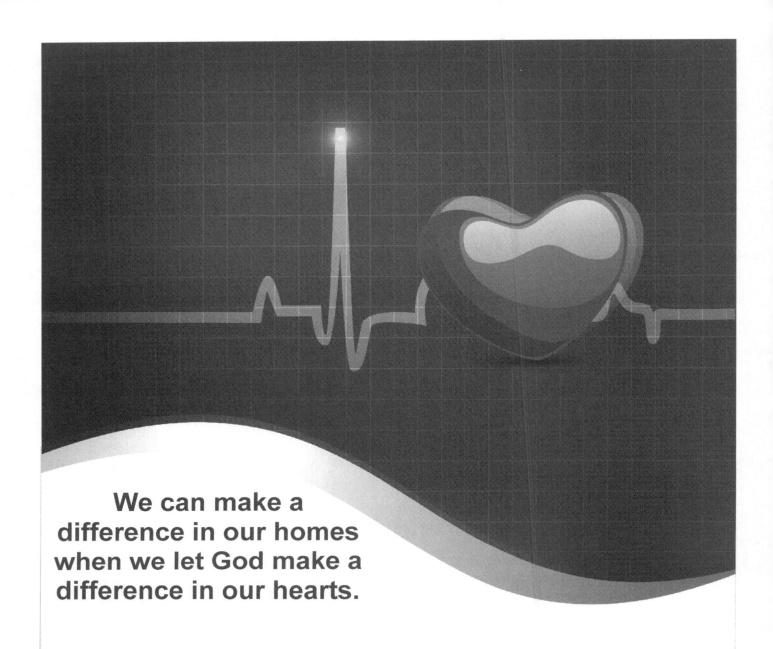

We can make a difference in our homes when we let God make a difference in our hearts.

Above all else, guard your heart, for it is the wellspring of life.

Proverbs 4:23 (NIV)

Made in the
USA
Columbia, SC